Unseen Upton Si

Unseen Upton Sinclair

Nine Unpublished Stories, Essays and Other Works

UPTON SINCLAIR

edited by
Ruth Clifford Engs

McFarland & Company, Inc., Publishers
Jefferson, North Carolina, and London

Frontispiece: Upton Sinclair, ca. 1909.

Upton Sinclair's writings — "Suffragetteland"; "One Woman's Fight";
"Emancipated Husband"; "An Unmarried Mother"; "Eugenic Celibate
Motherhood"; "An Experimental Honeymoon"; "The Health Hunters: A
Farce Comedy in Four Acts"; "Restore and Keep Your Health by
Controlling Emotions"; "Little Algernon fragments" — are copyright
© 2009 John Weidman and Jeffrey Weidman. Reprinted with permission
of McIntosh & Otis, Inc.

Photographs of Upton Sinclair, Meta F. Sinclair, and Mary Craig K.
Sinclair courtesy of Lilly Library, Indiana University, Bloomington.

LIBRARY OF CONGRESS CATALOGUING-IN-PUBLICATION DATA

Sinclair, Upton, 1878–1968.
    Unseen Upton Sinclair : nine unpublished stories, essays and other
works / Upton Sinclair ; edited by Ruth Clifford Engs.
        p.   cm.
    Includes bibliographical references and index.

    ISBN 978-0-7864-4518-9
    softcover : 50# alkaline paper ∞

    I. Engs, Ruth Clifford.   II. Title.
    PS3537.I85A6   2009
    818'.5209 — dc22   2009025958

British Library cataloguing data are available

Writings of Upton Sinclair ©2009 John Weidman and Jeffrey Weidman;
all other contents ©2009 Ruth Clifford Engs. All rights reserved

Cover photograph: Upton Sinclair, ca. 1906 (courtesy Lilly Library, Indiana
University, Bloomington, Indiana)

Manufactured in the United States of America

McFarland & Company, Inc., Publishers
    Box 611, Jefferson, North Carolina 28640
    www.mcfarlandpub.com

For Bill Engs

Acknowledgments

Few publications are accomplished entirely by one individual. Many others generally assist in its birth. This collection would not have been possible without the help of several individuals. I would like to thank Megan Cole and Andrew Kotylo who meticulously transcribed the Sinclair manuscripts into electronic files. I am indebted to the staff of the Lilly Library for their aid in many aspects of this book. These individuals include: Breon Mitchell, Sue Presnell, Martin Joachim, Gabriel Swift, Zach Downey, Erika Dowell, David Frasier, Penny Ramon, and the reading room student assistants. My deepest thanks goes to Saundra Taylor, Curator of Lilly Library Manuscripts; Rebecca Cape, head of the Lilly Library reading room; and Jeffrey Graf, reference librarian at the Indiana University Wells Library, for reading and critiquing the manuscript.

I am especially grateful to the copyright holders John and Jeffrey Weidman, their agent McIntosh and Otis, Inc. and the Lilly Library for permission to publish the manuscripts in this collection.

Most importantly, I would like to thank my academic unit, the Department of Applied Health Sciences, for its continued support of my research projects. Finally, I deeply indebted to my "emancipated husband," Jeffrey Franz, who always allows me the space for creative endeavors.

Table of Contents

Acknowledgments vii
Preface 1
Introduction: A Biography of Upton Sinclair 5

Part I: Woman Suffrage and Emancipation 41
ONE: Suffragetteland 43
TWO: One Woman's Fight 45
THREE: The Emancipated Husband: A One-Reel Comedy 55

Part II: Defying Sexual Convention 73
FOUR: An Unmarried Mother 75
FIVE: Eugenic Celibate Motherhood 91
SIX: An Experimental Honeymoon 105

Part III: Search for Health 133
SEVEN: The Health Hunters: A Farce Comedy in Four Acts . . . 135
EIGHT: Restore and Keep Your Health by Controlling
    Emotions. 145
NINE: "Little Algernon" Fragments 149

Bibliography 173
Index 175

[I will] tell you things that may be useful to you in the brief span of your life ... [I'll] show you how to live, how to find health and happiness and success, how to work and how to play, how to eat and how to sleep, how to love and to marry. — Upton Sinclair, *The Book of Life*, 1922

Preface

In 2006, I began to explore the hypothesis that Upton Sinclair was a typical Progressive Era health crusader — that is, an individual who campaigned for both personal and public health reforms ranging from fad diets to Prohibition. Much of my research has been carried out at the Lilly Library, Indiana University, Bloomington, Indiana, which holds the majority of Sinclair's papers and publications. Among them I found a few unpublished short stories, essays, sketches for plays, and a script. These works make up the body of this collection.[1]

Two themes emerge from these unpublished manuscripts — women seeking independence and defying sexual and social conventions, and individuals seeking diet and health systems to cure their various ailments; these themes are often linked together in the plot. A few manuscripts offer serious thoughts on these topics. Most are satires or comedies.

For over fifteen years, I have researched and written about Progressive Era health reform movements and reformers.[2] Sinclair's unpublished drafts address issues of health and social reform during this era. However, my primary research project will only use a summary of these works. Scholars seeking detailed information about the manuscripts for their own investigations have until now been at a disadvantage, as the material could only be examined in the reading room of the Lilly library.

Therefore, I thought it important to make these largely unknown works more available by publishing them as a collection. In print they will be more accessible and will more readily come to the attention of scholars, Sinclair aficionados, and the reading public. The publication of the drafts will aid academics in literature, history, sociology, political science, public health, and American studies who are researching Sinclair and the

1

history and culture of the Progressive Era. A further reason to publish these drafts is to save wear-and-tear on the increasingly fragile pages of the original manuscripts.

The dates, and even publication status, of the sketches, essays, fragments of stories and plays published here are largely unknown. To ascertain more details concerning these items, the Lilly Library collection and other sources were searched.[3] In particular, I explored annotated bibliographies of all of Sinclair's works. These included John Ahouse's *Upton Sinclair: A Descriptive Annotated Bibliography* (1994), Ronald Gottesman's *Upton Sinclair: An Annotated Checklist* (1973), and Gottesman and Charles L. P. Silet's *The Literary Manuscripts of Upton Sinclair* (1972). These authors note that for seven of the nine manuscripts, publication is uncertain or the item was not published. Two manuscripts, "Eugenic Celebrated Motherhood" and "An Experimental Honeymoon," were not mentioned in their publications.

To discover clues as to where and when drafts might have been composed, I searched the biographies of Sinclair, including Anthony Arthur's *Radical Innocent: Upton Sinclair* (2006), Ivan Scott's *Upton Sinclair: The Forgotten Socialist* (1997), William A. Bloodworth's *Upton Sinclair* (1977); Leon A. Harris's *Upton Sinclair, An American Rebel* (1975), Jon A. Yoder's *Upton Sinclair* (1975), and Floyd Dell's *Upton Sinclair: A Study in Social Protest* (1927). Little information was found.

In addition, I also examined Sinclair's autobiographical writings and the autobiographical novels of his close friends. These works included: *The Autobiography of Upton Sinclair* (1962); *Love's Pilgrimage* (1911), based upon his and Meta Fuller's unhappy marriage; Fuller's unpublished autobiographical novel, *Thyrsis and Corydon*; Harry Kemp's *Tramping on Life* (1922); and *Southern Belle*, the autobiography of Sinclair's second wife, Mary Craig Kimbrough.

Based upon the content in these works, Sinclair likely wrote the manuscripts — with the exception of two — during the final years of his first marriage and the beginning years of his second, around 1910 to 1915. "Eugenic Celibate Motherhood" and "Restore and Keep Your *Health* by Controlling Emotions" were probably written between 1918 and 1920. Sinclair wrote the three drafts concerning the British suffrage movement in 1912, and may have reworked them in 1913. On April 11, 1912, Sinclair mentions in a letter to his second wife, Craig, that he had met many individuals active in the British movement and had written some "hot stuff for them." Only one item, "An Unmarried Mother," had a date (1915) and place (Gulfport, Mississippi) noted on it.

Since the publication of these nine drafts is a peripheral to my primary research on Upton Sinclair, I will not comment on the literary merit of the manuscripts or speculate in detail as to why they were not published. Perhaps editors did not consider them of interest to their reading public. A few may have been too scandalous for the time. Sinclair himself, after consideration, may have not thought them worthy, or did not wish to waste any more time perusing their publication. One ("An Experimental Honeymoon") appears to be Sinclair's own internal debate over whether or not he wished to marry again after his divorce. A limited search of correspondence between Sinclair and some editors did not find anything that had addressed these manuscripts. Sinclair frequently self-published books that mainstream publishing houses would not accept. Why he did not publish these short manuscripts, or develop the two proposed theatrical scripts, is a mystery for other scholars to solve.

The manuscripts were transcribed as written. The transcripts include corrections or editing by Sinclair, or possibly other hands. Obvious typographical errors, however, were corrected. In a few instances, page-long paragraphs were broken up for ease of reading. The manuscripts range in length from two to forty-eight pages, double spaced. One manuscript is incomplete, but is included in the collection as it provides information about Sinclair's opinions on health and social issues.

The present work begins with an introduction in the form of a brief biography of Upton Sinclair, focusing primarily on the years the manuscripts were written. The nine unpublished manuscripts follow, and are grouped into three parts based upon the subject matter. An editor's note precedes each selection.

Part I, Woman Suffrage and Emancipation, includes a sketch for a comedy, a short story, and the complete dialogue for a one act play. In the two plays, Sinclair pokes fun at suffragettes and supposedly independent women. In the short story, however, he portrays a more sober side of the Woman Suffrage Movement.

Part II, Defying Sexual Convention, includes two short stories and one essay. They would have been considered shocking and scandalous to some middle-class readers of the early twentieth century. Today, the subjects of single parenthood, artificial insemination, and cohabitation are commonplace — although still controversial in some segments of society. Sinclair depicts the ambivalence of women who want to be independent, as opposed to being adored and taken care of by a man. These works also point out the sexual double-standard between men and women, and between socio-economic classes.

Part III, Search for Health, is the most amusing section of the collection. Sinclair was beset by stomach problems, what he called "dyspepsia." To treat this disabling problem, he tried many diet and treatment regimes. He finally came to the conclusion that a dietary fast was the best cure for his ailment. With his knowledge of numerous cures, he satirizes the lucrative business of health and religious gurus who fleece the rich and famous in a sketch for a comedy, and again in unpublished installment fragments of his serialized novel, *The Health of Little Algernon.*

Notes

1. With the exception of Chapter Nine, the other chapters are "stand-alone" works. Nine is composed of two unpublished installments for the serialized novel, *The Health of Little Algernon*, published in *Physical Culture*, 1911–1912. Two items are brief sketches for theatrical comedy productions.

2. Engs, Ruth Clifford. *The Eugenics Movement: An Encyclopedia* (2005); Engs, *The Progressive Era's Health Reform Movement* (2003); Engs, *Clean Living Movements: American Cycles of Health Reform* (2000).

3. The Lilly Library has several lists from the Upton Sinclair Manuscripts Collection. Some can be found online: http://www.indiana.edu/~liblilly/lilly/mss/subfile/ sinclrwrit2.html

Introduction: A Biography of Upton Sinclair

This biographical sketch of Upton Sinclair focuses on the years 1900 through 1915. During this era, his writings — both published and unpublished — reflect issues of marital relationships, ideals of woman suffrage and independence, diet and food fanaticism, and a search for treatments to cure his, and his first wife's, ailments. These issues are the themes of the nine manuscripts contained in this volume. Both Sinclair's first (Meta H. Fuller) and second (Mary Craig Kimbrough) wives took the last name Sinclair. To avoid confusion, Meta and Craig will be used, respectively, for these two women. Both wives influenced the choice of topics of his writings, particularly during the time period of this collection.

Prior to 1900: Childhood and Family

Upton Beall Sinclair, Jr., was born, September 20, 1878, in Baltimore, Maryland. Both sides of his family came from the declining Southern aristocracy. His father, Upton Beall Sinclair, was from an old Virginia naval family that traced its linage to officers in the British navy; they supposedly were direct descendants of Robert the Bruce of Scotland. His great-grandfather fought in the first American naval battle after the Revolution. Sinclair's male ancestors had fought in the Confederate Navy.

His mother, Priscilla Harden Sinclair, was descended from a "dozen French kings." Her father, John S. Harden, was Secretary-Treasurer of the Western Maryland Railroad. Sinclair's aunt — on his mother's side — married John Randolph Bland, founder of the United States Fidelity and Guaranty Company. As a child, when his father had squandered his wages on alcohol, Sinclair and his mother often lived with this aunt and uncle.

Sinclair's father had worked as a wholesale liquor salesman, and a representative for a straw-hat manufacturer. When Sinclair was nine or ten, the family moved to New York City. Here his father sold men's clothing, spent a lot of time in saloons drinking and "treating" his customers, and often depleted all of his earnings. The young Sinclair was sometimes sent by his mother to search the saloons for his drunken father. This "made an indelible impression" on him as a child. Sinclair had other relatives who were alcoholic; some committed suicide.[1]*

The senior Sinclair's alcoholism often caused the family to be impoverished. The young Upton lived in conditions ranging from bug-ridden boarding houses to the fine houses of his mother's wealthy relatives. Sinclair relates that this background set the stage for "other eccentricities of mine besides my belief in Prohibition."[2] Sinclair's mother, very pious and puritanical, abhorred alcohol, coffee, tea, and tobacco. Sinclair followed her example and abstained from alcohol and "stimulants" throughout his lifetime.

One boarding house (Weisiger House) — where the family resided for a couple of winters in New York City — catered to old Southern families. Here, Sinclair met Meta Fuller, who later became his first wife.[3] Both his mother, Priscilla, and Meta's mother, Mary Fuller, became friends, and began to vacation together. Meta's father, William, had been a newspaper reporter and then became deputy clerk of court in New York City. Over time, the Fullers moved from the boarding house to better accommodations.

As a child, Sinclair escaped into books to get away from the turmoil between his parents and his "sordid surroundings." This made him a self-described "dreamer." His mother read to him as a child, and he "taught himself to read at the age of five, before anyone realized what was happening."[4] He received books from his relatives for Christmas and read prodigiously. In the stories he read, he found a favorite theme for his later writing, namely "the contrast between the social classes; there are characters from both worlds, the rich and the poor, and the plots contrive to carry you from one to the other."[5]

Sinclair constantly described his father as weak and a poor role model;

See Notes beginning on page 36.

however, he found fatherly support from two clergymen. His mother, to maintain her southern aristocratic status, always went to the most fashionable church in the neighborhood. At the Church of the Holy Communion, Sinclair met the Rev. William W. Moir, who took Sinclair — and about fifty other boys — under his wing. Sinclair became a devout Episcopalian and even taught Sunday school for a year. As an older youth, he became an agnostic, left the Episcopal Church, and attended the local Unitarian Church. Here he met Minot J. Savage, its minister. Both Moir and Savage helped Sinclair during his early marriage and writing career.

Sinclair did not go to school until he was ten years old because of concern that "his mind was outgrowing his body."[6] When he was finally enrolled in public school, he was very advanced for his age — other than in arithmetic. Sinclair went through eight years of grammar school in less than two years. He was now ready to go to City College of New York — a combination high school and college that awarded a bachelor's degree after five years of work. However, he was too young to enter and was required to attend a grammar school for another year. In 1892, at age thirteen, he entered the college, and in 1897 graduated in the middle of his class. His uncle, Terry Sinclair, offered him an appointment to the Naval Academy at Annapolis. Sinclair notes in his autobiography, "this was regarded as my birthright, but I declined it."[7] He had made up his mind to become a lawyer.

Sinclair's summers as a child and youth were spent at the country home of the Bland family, or with his mother at resorts in Virginia while his father was on the road. If his father was not drinking, they stayed at a nice place. During his late teenage years, when he wrote "half-dime novels," Sinclair spent summers at places in the north. These included the home of an old sea captain on the St. Lawrence River in Canada, an isolated cabin, and a hotel on a lake in the Adirondacks. The wilderness experiences, and many canoeing trips, gave him color for several of his later works. He also found the quiet and isolation conducive for writing, a practice he maintained for the rest of his life.

Sinclair became a "hack" writer, around age 14. He wrote ethnic jokes and stories for pulp fiction publications — inexpensive magazines or novels made of newsprint or poor quality paper. This led him into writing army and navy adventures for boys. Sinclair wrote under both the name Ensign Clark Fitch, USN, and Lieutenant Frederick Garrison, USA, for these tales. In addition, he wrote stories about the Spanish-American War (February to December 1898) for another magazine. These potboilers were successful, and he was paid enough to take care of both his mother and himself. Sinclair bought and learned to play the violin, leading to a life-long enjoyment; tennis was another recreational passion. During this heavy writing period, two stenographers worked for him, and he wrote seven days a week.[8]

In 1897, Sinclair enrolled in Columbia University as a special student, so he could take any courses he wished. He did not study law and stayed only two years at the university. During the mornings, he attended lectures or played the violin. In the afternoons he dictated the potboilers, and in the evenings he edited the previous day's material. By being a hack writer, he learned to shape a story. At age twenty-one, Sinclair relates he became "obsessed with the desire to write a serious novel, I came to loathe this hack-work ... it was the end of my youth."[9]

1900 through 1915: Work, Health, and Women

In April 1900, Sinclair went to Lake Massawippi in Quebec, just over the New York border. He rented a small cabin through July to work on his first serious novel, which he called *Springtime and Harvest*. This novel concerns a young woman's choice between marrying a rich man whom she does not love, or a poor man whom she does. In August, he moved to a farmhouse and lived on an isolated island in Lake Placid until it became too cold. A poor French-Canadian family who lived up on the mountain-side brought him milk and eggs. He also encountered a golf links for the first time and thought the sport a waste of time. The Canadian family and the wastefulness of golf were later used in his serialized novel *The Health of Little Algernon* (1911–1912).

During the summer of 1900, his mother, her friend Mary Fuller, and her daughter, Meta, vacationed at the lake. Meta visited Sinclair at his cabin and he began to be her tutor and teacher. Meta had always wanted to go to college, but her father thought it unnecessary for a woman. Sin-clair taught her German and other subjects. They interacted on a daily basis and proceeded to fall in love. Both mothers were upset by the situ-ation; Meta's mother hastily spirited her away to another resort. Meta was inexperienced and immature for her age, and considered far too young for a serious relationship.

Sinclair returned to New York City in the fall when *Springtime and Harvest* had been completed. He solicited several publishers, but his manuscript was rejected. Since Sinclair considered himself a genius whose voice should be heard, he was unwilling to give up on the novel. He then "wrote a potboiler, earned a couple hundred dollars, and borrowed another two hundred from my uncle," and printed the book on his own.[10] From the sales, he earned just enough to pay back his uncle. This pattern of self-publishing was repeated over his lifetime. If a regular publishing house would not publish his work, he published it himself. This was particularly true for those later works that criticized American institutions such as the press, big business, religion and education.

Back in New York City, he spent much time with Meta. He continued to teach her German and introduced her to literature. He wanted her to be "a perfect woman."[11] As part of their courtship, she played the piano while he played the violin. Because of the pressure of both families against their relationship, they eloped and were married by the Unitarian minister, the Rev. Minot J. Savage, at the Church of the Messiah, October 17, 1900. Both mothers were most unhappy with the situation, each thinking the other's child not a suitable match for her own child. After the marriage, Upton and Meta lived with Sinclair's parents in a small room.

During the early twentieth century the teaching of birth control was illegal, even for physicians. Sexuality and contraception were not readily discussed in "polite society." Both Meta and Sinclair were naive. Sinclair did consult his family physician about preventing pregnancy, and he recommended the rhythm method. However, "it turned out that his knowledge had not been adequate," and Meta found herself pregnant in April 1901.[12] It was an "inopportune time to have a child." Meta tried various nostrums and over-exercise to create a miscarriage.[13] They also visited several physicians to learn how to "thwart the ways of nature." Because abortions were illegal and very dangerous in this era, Meta decided against it.[14]

In June 1901, Sinclair and the pregnant Meta traveled to Leek Island in the Thousand Islands. He set up a tent platform and "began the back-to-nature life" again in an isolated area so he could write. He worked on a new novel, *Prince Hagen*. This tale is about a prince of the Wagnerian underworld, a kind of arch-capitalist, who goes to New York City to gain power and wealth. Meta in her pregnancy felt isolated, and Sinclair was often bad tempered when interrupted. In the autumn, they returned to New York City. However, they were impoverished; their only funds were $25 a month from Meta's family. Meta went to live with her parents.

In the meantime Funk and Wagnalls agreed to reissue *Springtime and Harvest* as *King Midas*, which was released in the fall of 1901. In this work, Sinclair, for the first time, wrote under the name of Upton Sinclair, rather that Upton B. Sinclair, Jr. However, the book did not sell well, and the publisher, along with several others, was not interested in *Prince Hagen*.

On December 1, 1901, David Sinclair was born. The experience of Meta's labor and delivery is related in *Love's Pilgrimage* (1911), a story of their relationship written in 1910 when the marriage was in its final stage of disintegration. Meta and the baby lived with her parents, who refused to let Sinclair visit his son until he was employed in a "real job." Sinclair "lived in a garret room, and haunted publishers and editors, and wrote potboilers."[15] He sold a few sketches, book reviews, and juvenile adventure books but barely survived during that winter. Meta would secretly come to visit him in his room with the baby and walk up long exhausting flights of stairs, which she blamed for the health problems she would suffer later in life.

During the summer of 1902, Meta lived with her parents in the Catskills, and Sinclair went alone to Leek Island, where he and Meta had spent the previous summer. Sinclair's anger and depression at not being able to find a publisher for his books was reflected in his new work, *The Journal of Arthur Sterling*. This semi-autobiographical novel is the story of the suicide of a brilliant young poet who had composed an epic poem that no one wanted to publish. Like Sinclair, the protagonist believes he is a genius who should be published, but continues to encounter insensitive publishers. On June 9, 1902, Sinclair arranged for a friend to send an obituary of Arthur Sterling to a New York paper. Other friends caused a stir in the news media to set the stage for the book. After he finished the novel, he went to the Adirondacks, where he met the literary advisor of D. Appleton and Company, who agreed to publish the book even though it was a hoax.

Sinclair wrote the novel in six weeks working fourteen-hour days. This concentrated effort destroyed "both mind and body." He developed stomach problems, which had plagued him the previous summer while working on his first novel.[16] This "dyspepsia" caused by stress and overwork was to remain with Sinclair the rest of his life. Over the years he sought and experimented with many cures, most of which appear in his satires, including one sketch for a stage play, "The Health Hunters," found in this volume. After the attack of pain, he consulted a local country doctor and was told to take "a spoonful of pink liquid containing pig pepsin." However, the remedy only worked for a while and he "found it necessary to become [his] own doctor and another kind of 'crank.'"[17]

In the fall of 1902, after finishing *Arthur Sterling*, he met a socialist writer, Leonard D. Abbott, who worked for Funk and Wagnalls, the publisher of his *King Midas*. Abbot in turn introduced Sinclair to

Meta Fuller Sinclair, ca. 1898.

George Herron, a socialist and former Episcopal priest, who became a lifelong friend. Sinclair corresponded with Herron, who invited him for dinner in November 1902. At this dinner he met Gaylord Wilshire, a wealthy socialist who would play a part in Sinclair's life over the next decade (Wilshire Boulevard in Los Angeles is named after Gaylord Wilshire).

After this meeting, and studying socialistic literature, Sinclair was converted to the philosophy. Socialism underlay both his fictional and non-fictional works for several decades. Socialism at this point in history was a populist movement with roots among Midwest farmers. It was not connected to the Marxism and violence later advocated by V.I. Lenin.[18] Sinclair became so enthused with the movement as the only answer to social justice and capitalist corruption that shortly before he completed *The Jungle*, he helped found the Intercollegiate Socialist Society. On September 12, 1905, the society was founded with fellow socialist Jack London, the novelist, as its first president.

During the winter of 1903, Sinclair had little money. He lived in a rooming house with his alcoholic father and alcoholic maternal uncle. Sinclair's writings became infused with socialistic propaganda. In his next novel, *Captain of Industry*, Sinclair portrayed a greedy capitalist who manipulates the stock market, and dies an inglorious death. However, the book failed to interest publishers, and was not issued until December, 1906, after *The Jungle* had caused a sensation.

In February 1903, the supposed journal of the dead poet Arthur Sterling was published, to some favorable reviews. When it was found to be a hoax, Sinclair was condemned by several critics, and the work did not sell well. However, this publication gave Sinclair the publicity he craved. Sinclair rebutted the negative comments from his critics in a manifesto concerning starving writers, "My Cause," in *The Independent*, May 14, 1903. In this essay he describes himself as a "penniless rat" and mentions that he now planned to concentrate his energies on writing a historical novel about the Civil War.

Sinclair had given George Herron a copy of *Arthur Sterling*, and Herron had liked it. Sinclair visited him, explained his impoverished situation, and asked for a loan to write *Manassas*. Herron agreed, and in May 1903 Sinclair, along with Meta and their baby, David, moved to an isolated space on a farm near Princeton University. The university's Civil War collection, the second largest in the country, was necessary for his research. He spent two years collecting data and writing the work.

On the rented property, Sinclair established a campsite with a large tent. He set up a smaller tent in a more secluded area for writing. In June 1903, the novel *Prince Hagen* was finally accepted, bringing some needed money to Sinclair. With this money he had a small cabin built to replace the larger tent. Sinclair named the cabin the "soap box." During the previous winter, baby David had been diagnosed with rickets — a lack of Vitamin D which can cause deformed bones. Their physician prescribed a special dietary regimen. It took much time for Meta to prepare the food, which required grinding meat, chopping chicken bones, and mixing them with cream and milk, which was then boiled for hours.[19]

Sinclair spent much of the day gathering data for his book at the Princeton University library, and then isolated himself in his tent to write.

Because of fear of another pregnancy, Sinclair and Meta attempted to live like "brother and sister"—even sleeping in separate beds in the inadequately heated cabin during the winter. It was a difficult life for Meta and their relationship slowly disintegrated. In the household "he made the laws and he and Meta lived according to them." Sinclair repeatedly told Meta that he was a "thinking machine" and that she was oversexed. Meta, in her unpublished autobiography, writes that Sinclair "was inclined to relegate sex impulses to the limbo of unrestrained human emotions along with drunkenness, wife-beating, etc." As a lover she suggests, "He was like a monk who occasionally threw aside his cassock to try to assume the role of lover for a brief space."[20]

During the winter, David developed pneumonia and almost died. This trauma, in addition to a lack of sexual activity and emotional comfort, along with loneliness, caused Meta to become increasingly depressed and "nervous." One night Sinclair found her sobbing with a revolver in her hand. "She had been trying for hours to get up the courage to put a bullet into her head."[21] She also became physically sick with numerous pains which may have been appendicitis, or severe menstrual cramps. Sick and unhappy, Meta and David returned to her parents' home in New York City, where she could find emotional support, for the rest of the winter.

In the spring of 1904, Meta moved back to the small cabin, and Sinclair finished *Manassas*. The story relates the life of a young southerner, Allen Montague, who grew up in the North and embraces the Abolitionist cause. It was supposed to be the first book of a trilogy, but it ends with the Battle of Bull Run—also called the First Battle of Manassas.[22] The manuscript was promptly accepted by Macmillan and published in August 1904. Sinclair's articles were now being accepted by some magazines and his life appeared to be on the upswing.

Since Sinclair was now "supporting his wife," his father-in-law invited him, in the summer of 1904, on a canoe trip in northern Ontario.[23] The experiences surrounding canoeing, portaging, and camping, like his previous backwoods experiences, were used in the satire *The Health of Little Algernon.*

Although *Manassas* won critical praise, it sold fewer than two thousand copies. The editor of *Appeal to Reason*, a socialist magazine, liked it and proposed an idea for another book. In *Manassas*, Sinclair had portrayed "the struggle over chattel slavery" and now the editor wanted the same thing for "wage slavery," and a particular concern was the Chicago stock-yards. In October 1904, Sinclair went to the stockyards as an undercover investigative reporter to examine conditions in the meat packing industry.

In the meantime, he was concerned by Meta's emotional and physical health. He met with the clergyman who had married them, the Reverend Savage, and discussed with him Meta's depression, near suicide the previous winter, and the need for a larger house. With a loan from the clergyman, Sinclair bought a sixty-acre farm with a large farmhouse near Princeton.

While Sinclair was collecting data from the Chicago slaughterhouses, Meta had another operation and "a long distressing illness from which she nearly died." She was hospitalized for several weeks.[24] During this hospital stay she "fell in love" with a young doctor who cared for her. She related the experience to Sinclair — they had agreed not to keep secrets from each other. He was not happy with this revelation and was likely not aware that it was not uncommon for lonely female patients to fall in love with their male physicians.

Before Sinclair started to write about the conditions of the Chicago slaughterhouse workers, he, along with Meta and their son David, moved to the farm. A nurse also moved in with the family to care for Meta, whose recovery was slow. Sinclair transported the small cabin that he had built the previous winter to the farm as his writing place.

On Christmas Day, 1904, Sinclair began to write *The Jungle*, and worked on it continuously for three months. He poured his own experiences of poverty, family illnesses, and his son's near death the previous winter into the characters of the fiction. The stress from this intensive writing caused such severe stomach pains that he found it difficult to write. A relative offered him a brief respite in the South. After a couple of weeks in Florida, he came back refreshed and worked again on the book through the summer of 1905.

Sinclair approached several publishers, but they rejected *The Jungle* as they thought it too raw. In the meantime, beginning in February of 1905, the serialized version of the book began to appear in *Appeal to Reason*. Doubleday, Page and Company finally accepted the manuscript, and it was published as a book in February, 1906. Although Sinclair was attempting to show the plight of slaughterhouse workers to gain sympathy for socialism, the book caused revulsion against the meat industry. President Theodore Roosevelt had the claims investigated and found them accurate.

The Jungle immediately put Sinclair in the limelight of controversy, and he was now classified as a "muckraker," a writer who delighted in digging up dirt (the term was coined by Roosevelt). The book became a major factor in the passage of the Pure Food and Drug Laws and the Meat Inspection Act of 1906. It also brought him needed funds.[25] A hundred years later, *The Jungle* is the one book for which Sinclair is still noted, although he wrote almost 90 books over his long career.[26]

Meta remained on the farm, isolated and sick. A friend introduced her to Christian Science, which brought her some relief. However, Sinclair was so opposed to the practice that she gave it up; her pains then returned.[27] Sinclair sent her to Florida, and David went to live with Meta's mother. While in Florida Meta met a young man and "fell in love" with him; she related this emotional relationship to Sinclair, which led to further deterioration of their marriage.[28]

Sinclair was not always wise when it came to finances. He wanted to "spend his money for the uplifting of mankind." A part of the socialist philosophy was a belief in cooperation and the idea that an individual home was wasteful and extravagant. Sinclair now had a fairly large amount of money ($30,000, which in 2008 would be around $700,000) from *The Jungle*. On June 4, 1906, he outlined a plan for a "home colony" in *The Independent*. He and a group of intellectuals, socialists, and "bohemians" agreed to form a community, or "co-operative home." Sinclair bought an old boys school overlooking Englewood, New Jersey. A company was formed and stock was issued, although Sinclair owned most of the shares.

Sinclair had hoped that with less isolation Meta would be happier. On November 1, 1906, the group moved into Helcion Hall, or the "Helcion Home Community"—nicknamed H.H. Community residents included Michael Williams, with whom Sinclair later collaborated to write a book. Among other residents were the budding writer Sinclair Lewis, a Yale student, who worked as a janitor, several Columbia University professors and their families, and various artists and writers.

It was a happy experience for Meta, who became more independent. This was upsetting to Sinclair, who was used to having his way even in the domestic sphere. In addition, Sinclair and a wife of a Columbia professor, Anna Noyes, had an "experimental affair" which lasted a couple of weeks. Sinclair espoused "open marriage," and "trial marriages." Both concepts, lumped together as "free love," were against the sexual convention of the time.[29] In the minds of the press, "Free love and H.H. became synonymous though how much it deserved this reputation is uncertain."[30]

Various people came to visit the community, including John Dewey, the educator, and William James, the psychologist. Armistead Collier, a married mystic poet, visited, and he and Meta became emotionally involved. He wrote Meta — his "Ole Tiger eye princess" — for several years. Sinclair was jealous of this relationship, even though he had engaged in his own "experimental" sexual affair. Sinclair, later, in many works wrote against the double standard of sexuality, although it could be questioned if, on an emotional level, he actually subscribed to it.

Alas, tragedy struck the community. On March 7, 1907, Helicon Hall mysteriously burned down in the middle of the night. All the residents escaped with the exception of an itinerant carpenter, who had been too drunk to leave. The insurance paid only about a third of the value of the property. Most importantly — for historical research — Sinclair's papers, unless they were in the hands of publishers, were destroyed in the fire. Inasmuch as he owned most of the community's stock, he was responsible for paying back the debts. Sinclair remarks, "every dollar of the debts of Helicon Home Colony was paid," but their payment caused him financial distress.[31]

After the tragedy, in the winter of 1907, Sinclair and Meta lived with Gay and Mary Wilshire in New York City. Meta "became pregnant which proved a source of worry to them both." It was "a terrible moment in which to conceive a child, and subsequently the doctors felt she was in no condition to bear one." Meta "went to the hospital for further surgical treatment."[32] Sinclair later noted, in 1910, that Meta had "undergone three major surgical operations and had several serious illnesses" in a five-year period.[33] The surgeries involved at least one abortion and possibly the removal of a tumor or appendix. After the surgery, they moved to Point Pleasant, New Jersey, with a secretary and a maid.

A few weeks later, Meta developed peritonitis from either a misdiagnoses of appendicitis or as a result of the abortion, and almost died.[34] Sinclair claimed he pulled her back to life by "urging her to live, to keep holding on; and that voice came to her as something commanding, stirring new energies in her soul."[35] By this point she was suffering "from a complete nervous and mental breakdown."[36]

Because of her extreme illness, in August 1907, Sinclair sent her to John Harvey Kellogg's Battle Creek Sanitarium — called the San — accompanied by her mother and an old physician friend of the family. David was taken care of by the maid and secretary at Point Pleasant. Sinclair "went to the Adirondacks to rest" and to finish *The Metropolis*. Most of his works up to this point had focused on workers and the poor; this novel portrayed the rich, and how they lived.

After he finished writing the book, Sinclair went to Keene Valley, New York, and spent a week at the utopian community of Prestonia Mann Martin and her English husband John Martin, one of the founders of the British socialist Fabian Society. They also supported women's suffrage. Just before World War I, while in England, Sinclair met them again and was introduced to British suffragettes. These two meetings influenced his later writings on the emancipation of women, including the three works in Part II.

While in the Adirondacks, in August 1907, Sinclair lived on rice, beans, prunes, bacon and fish but no fresh fruit or vegetables; he suffered from constipation and headaches and began to read about cures for his health conditions. In the fall of that year, he visited Meta at the San. While there he learned about diets, water cures and vegetarianism as possible cures for his own "unruly" stomach. Experiences with these treatments converted Sinclair into a "food fanatic." He adopted a strict vegetarian diet hoping it would cure his "dyspepsia" even under the pressure of intense writing. Sinclair tried this diet for the next three years and claimed it made him feel better. After he had adopted fasting in 1909 as "the only" dietary regimen, he satirized many of the cures used at the Battle Creek Sanitarium in his writings, including two works in the present work. This mockery led to a falling out between Sinclair and Kellogg.[37]

At the San, Meta briefly met Alfred Kuttner, a Harvard graduate student, with whom — with Sinclair's blessings — she had an affair in the summer of 1910. Sinclair again met Michael Williams, a socialist writer and one of the Helicon Hall colonists. Williams was attempting to cure his alcoholism at the institution. The two men decided to write a book on their health experiences.

To carry out this project and to give him company, Sinclair invited Williams to join him in Bermuda, where he had rented a large isolated house for the winter. In December 1907, Sinclair and David, along with the Williams family and an assortment of other people, traveled to Bermuda. Sinclair mandated a strict vegetarian diet for everyone in the household. Meta was released from the San, as her health had improved. She joined Sinclair in January 1908, and they worked on their relationship. However, she and Sinclair argued about food and the diet that Sinclair had imposed on everyone.

While in Bermuda, Williams focused on his autobiographical novel, *The High Romance*. Sinclair worked on *The Millennium*, a satirical science-fiction play of the future in which only ten individuals survive a chemical-nuclear annihilation and begin a new civilization. It was not immediately accepted for publication.[38]

Sinclair and Williams collaborated on *Good Health and How We Won It*. Williams wrote most of the book, and Sinclair wrote the foreword. The book promoted the health advice of Kellogg's Battle Creek sanitarium, yogurt for longevity, daily exercise, a vegetarian diet, avoidance of stimulants and alcohol, and the general health advice of Progressive Era health reformers and fanatics.[39] Williams went back to New York to find a publisher in the spring of 1908. Sinclair and Williams, however, had a permanent falling out when Williams did not share the advance from the publisher with Sinclair. The book was published in 1909.

Sinclair returned to New York City in the spring. *The Metropolis*, published in March 1908, did not sell well. Sinclair began to work on a sequel, *The Moneychangers*, another novel of big business and Wall Street corruption. He received an advance and rented a little camp on Lake Placid, New York. Sinclair, Meta and David, their maid, and a young Seventh-day Adventist woman friend of Meta stayed at the camp. H.G. Wells, the British novelist, visited Sinclair for several weeks, and they enjoyed each others' company.

Meta attempted various types of mental healing to cure her continuing pains. At the camp, arguments continued between Meta and Sinclair over the strict vegetarian diet that he imposed on the whole household. The health of all suffered from these dietary experiments. David, at one point, while traveling with his father, rebelled against this regimen, and secretly ate a ham sandwich on a train. Sinclair severely whipped him for this transgression.[40] Arguments between Sinclair and Meta over food and diet were another factor in the unraveling of their marriage.

The Moneychangers was published in the fall of 1908. Sinclair, however, after the intense writing and constant arguments with Meta, "was close to a nervous breakdown, and had to get away from a most unhappy domestic situation, and take a complete rest."[41] He traveled to California to visit Gaylord Wilshire, who now owned a gold mine, and to see George Sterling, the poet. On the way he stopped in Lawrence, Kansas, to meet the "box-car poet," Harry Kemp, whom Sinclair considered "the coming poet of America." Kemp was a student at the state university. The two become friends. He also stopped at Reno, Nevada, because he and Meta were seriously discussing divorce. Reno was one of the few places in the United States where it was easy to obtain one.

Sinclair visited Wilshire's gold mine and then went to Carmel, an artist colony, where he visited Sterling. Sinclair was loaned a cottage for two months and felt at peace. While there he experimented with additional dietary regimes. He tried a "raw-food diet" where he "ate two meals a day, of nuts, fruits, olives and salad vegetables." To this he added shredded-wheat biscuits and graham crackers — the only cooked food. His stomach pains went away, but, he did note in his autobiography that he was not doing "nerve-destroying labor of creative writing." He rode horses, played tennis and met with Sterling and other friends. During this visit, Sinclair sadly realized that Sterling was an alcoholic. Although he had seen his father and male relatives drunk, this was the first time he had "seen a great mind distorted by alcohol."[42]

During this idyllic time in California, Sinclair wrote three one-act plays, produced them, and lost money. He was interviewed by newspapers. On January 30, 1909, the *San Francisco Examiner* ran a story with the headline "Sinclair sorry he is married to wife." It reported he thought "married women were slaves," and advocated trial marriage.

In the fall of 1908, Meta rented an apartment in New York City in which she "spent the four happiest months of her life."[43] In New York, Meta exerted her independence. She took singing lessons, studied music, and attended the theater and concerts with her mother. She also realized that she began to feel well for the first time since the birth of David. While in New York, Alfred Kuttner, whom she had met at Kellogg's Battle Creek establishment, began to write Meta. He had just returned from abroad and was on his way to Harvard for graduate work. They met briefly in New York and began an extensive exchange of letters.

Sinclair, in California, missed his wife and son. In April 1909, he asked her to pack up and join him in Florida, which she did. Meta notes several times in her unpublished autobiography, that throughout their marriage Sinclair had an approach versus avoidance mentality. When he was not with her, he wanted her. When he was with her, they were not happy. This mismatched relationship was partly due to the fact that he wanted to control all aspects of her life, while she wanted to gain independence.[44]

Sinclair rented a cottage in Coconut Grove, at that time a literary colony. While at the colony, he wrote a play, *The Machine*, a sequel to the *Moneychangers*. Sinclair and Meta again attempted to work on their marriage, but Meta and Kuttner continued to exchange letters. Sinclair was unhappy with this correspondence. However, Kuttner went to Europe again and the correspondences ceased.

For the summer of 1909, Sinclair rented a cottage on the shore in Cutchogue, Long Island. He hired a secretary and household assistant, Dave Howatt, who was a childhood friend of Harry Kemp. Howatt, a vegetarian, teetotaler, and nonsmoker, had spent time at Bernarr Macfadden's Physical Culture City near Outcalt (Helmetta), N.J. after being introduced to the vegetarian lifestyle by Kemp. Sinclair and his household experimented with the raw-food diet. Howatt coached Sinclair in various diets when his stomach began to rebel from the stress of overwork and domestic conflict. During this time Sinclair completed *Samuel the Seeker* (1910), a story about a "wise fool" who is abused by society but finally finds like-minded people — socialists.

By the end of the summer, Sinclair's health had greatly deteriorated. He had read Bernarr Macfadden's *Physical Culture* magazine on health and exercise. Macfadden recommended fasting for the treatment of many ailments. Sinclair wrote Macfadden about his problems and was invited, along with his family, to come to the institute for a fasting treatment in return for writing some articles.

The visit to Bernarr Macfadden's institution, in the autumn of 1909, became a pivotal point in Upton Sinclair's life in terms of his health, writings, and relationships. Sinclair became obsessed with fasting, and breaking the fast with a milk diet as the cure for his, and other people's, health problems. The treatment helped his stomach problems. Even David was put on a milk diet at the sanitarium. Sinclair's fanaticism and obsession with fasting and strange diets now became a compulsion. Over the next decade, diet and fasting themes emerged in many of his works.

At Battle Creek, the individuals who influenced the final dissolution of Sinclair and Meta's marriage converged. Meta met Harry Kemp. Sinclair and Meta met Mary Craig Kimbrough, a southerner, who was staying at Kellogg's institution across the street. The two women soon became fast friends. One of Sinclair's early biographers, Leon Harris, suggests that Craig possibly "began her plan to appropriate [Sinclair]" and that friendship with Meta was a means to this end. A more recent biographer, Ivan Scott, agrees.[45] Their friendship lasted through the early winter of 1912 when Sinclair was suing for a divorce from Meta, and was probably having a secret affair with Craig. It is interesting to note that Craig never mentions this friendship in her autobiography *Southern Belle,* which may have been written by Sinclair with Craig's input.[46]

In September 1909, Sinclair went to Fairhope, Alabama, a single-tax colony based upon the philosophy of Henry George. The cornerstone of George's philosophy was that land should be made available to those who would use it to produce or create. Only the land, and not the creative work or income from the land, would be taxed for community infrastructure and services. Sinclair rented a cottage on the bay front. David was sent to the Organic School, a progressive school in the colony. During this time, Sinclair ate a raw-food diet, fasted and engaged in vigorous daily exercise. Dave Howatt, now married and living in his own place, was again Sinclair's secretary.

Sinclair wrote a series of essays and satires concerning diet, health, cures, marriage, and relationships for Macfadden's *Physical Culture.* From October 1909 through August 1914, Sinclair's writings appeared almost monthly in the health magazine.

In two and a half days of continuous work, he wrote *The Nature-woman.* This comedy "sprang full-grown" into his brain and featured his idealized woman — one who was independent, promoted a healthy lifestyle of exercise and vegetarian diet, defied middle-class convention, and was knowledgeable of sexuality. The play was not successful. It was published in *Plays of Protest* in 1912.

In the meantime, Meta stayed at Macfadden's in the company of Craig for another month or so. Meta went to Fairhope in early 1910. When she arrived Sinclair suggested they write a semi-autobiographical novel of their marriage to be called *Love's Pilgrimage*. The hero and heroine, Thyrsis and Corydon respectively, were based upon the stock names of shepherds in classical Greek pastoral poetry.

The collaboration was to reflect the unhappiness within their marriage, but also to show an example of a couple who agreed to part and remain friends. Meta contributed to this work, and it contains many of their letters to each other. Sinclair suggested that a major factor in their unsuccessful marriage was that both of them, when they married, were ignorant of sexuality. That belief led him to strongly advocate "trial" or "experimental marriage."

In Fairhope, Sinclair insisted on a raw-food diet and dominated the household. As usual Meta chafed at the situation. In addition, Meta and Alfred Kuttner had begun to correspond again. Sinclair finally invited Alfred down to Fairhope — perhaps in an effort to encourage Alfred to marry Meta. Alfred came, but after much discussion, left in March to go back north. Several weeks later Meta returned to New York and moved into her parents' apartment. Alfred broke off the relationship and ceased writing, which greatly upset her. He suggested she see a Dr. A. A. Brill, his psychiatrist.[47]

Frank Stephens, head of another single-tax colony, in Arden, Delaware, about twenty miles from Philadelphia, invited Sinclair to live in his community. In April 1910, Sinclair and David went to Arden and remained there through early 1912. The colony was filled with socialists, artists, writers, bohemians, and "typical characters" of an artist colony. Since no bungalows were available, Sinclair rented a lot and installed three tents, one of them for Meta as she was not yet ready for a divorce.

At Arden, he finished *Love's Pilgrimage*, with Meta's input, and wrote the serialized novel *The Health of Little Algernon*, published in *Physical Culture* from December 1911 through June 1912. He also completed *The Fasting Cure*. This book was based upon two *Cosmopolitan* magazine articles, published in May 1910 and February 1911, along with some portions of articles contributed to *Physical Culture* magazine, and comments from readers. It appeared in print in March 1911.

Just before Sinclair left Fairhope for Arden, he met Dr. J. H. Salisbury, a meat-diet advocate. Sinclair now converted to an exclusive diet of "boiled beef and hot water" as a solution to most of the problems of the human body. He found he could do more work while on this diet compared to any other dietary systems he had tried. However, he felt like a "backslider" as he had been promoting a vegetarian diet for three years. This new diet system was rigidly enforced in Sinclair's household. It was far less ascetic than vegetarianism and did not appeal to Meta. Meta also exerted an independence with which Sinclair was uncomfortable. They vacillated between getting divorced and attempting to sort out the problems in their marriage.

At Arden, Sinclair hired a young secretary, Ellen Barrows, with whom Meta was friendly. In June 1910, Alfred Kuttner again started to correspond with Meta and with Sinclair. Sinclair agreed that Meta and Alfred should go away together and get the affair out of their system if she would "return to him."[48] The two went to the Adirondacks for a month in the summer of 1910 as a "trial honeymoon." However, the affair did not go well and Meta returned to Arden depressed. She believed Alfred had "homosexual tendencies."[49] After her return, Sinclair admitted to Meta that while she had been away, he had had an affair with his secretary, Ellen. Sinclair and Meta realized that a divorce was now inevitable, although both dreaded it.[50]

The publisher Mitchell Kennerley accepted *Love's Pilgrimage*. With an advance, Sinclair built a small two story cottage which was completed early in 1911. He was also getting paid for articles written for *Physical Culture*.

In the fall of 1910, Mary Craig Kimbrough traveled to New York to obtain help with her novel about Winnie Davis, the daughter of Jefferson Davis. Meta introduced her to various socialists, including the Wilshires. Sinclair briefly met Craig in New York City to discuss the project. In March 1911, Meta and Craig traveled to Gulfport, Mississippi.[51] While Meta was in Mississippi, Sinclair attended a gathering of the Intercollegiate Socialist Society in New York. At this meeting he met and fell in love with a young socialist worker, Inez Millholand, but denied he had an affair with her.

The year 1911 became one of the most traumatic in the life of Upton Sinclair. Meta and Craig came back north, in June, went to Arden and moved into Sinclair's newly built house.[52] However, "Almost immediately upon [Craig's] arrival there began a growing intimacy" between her and Sinclair.[53] This was not an open affair as had been the agreement throughout the Sinclairs' marriage. As a result Meta felt ignored, more isolated, and lonely.

Around the same time, Harry Kemp came to Arden. Shortly after his arrival, he and Meta began an affair. When Sinclair suspected or discovered this liaison, he asked Meta to leave. She and Craig went to New York to her parents' vacant apartment in early August; Harry soon followed. Meta's mother went to Arden to look after David. George Sterling came a week or so later and went to visit Meta at the Fullers' apartment. However, upon meeting Craig at the apartment, he immediately fell in love with her, and he felt that Meta did not like him. Over the next year, Sterling wrote Craig numerous letters and over a hundred sonnets, which Sinclair published eighteen years later, after Sterling had committed suicide. Since Sterling was married, he asked Craig to address her letters to him at his club or post boxes. He also destroyed Craig's letters to him.[54]

On August 23, 1911, Sinclair telegraphed his attorney to file for a divorce. A telegraph operator leaked this information to the press and a scandal broke out. *Love's Pilgrimage* had been published in May and was doing well until the newspapers printed news of the Meta and Kemp affair.[55]

To avoid the swarms of reporters that converged upon Meta's parents' apartment, Meta and Harry escaped to the New Jersey shore, and Craig went to a hotel.[56] Hoping to calm the media circus, Sinclair arranged with the press for Meta to give an interview to the newspapers during which she discussed her ideals of "sex independence of women," including the right of a woman to have a trial marriage. Upton Sinclair, Meta and Kemp were present at one interview.[57] The press had a field day. They suggested that Sinclair had "taught his wife free love and then repudiated her when she took him at his word." Sinclair included this bitter experience with the press in *The Brass Check* (1920).[58]

Meta and Kemp rented a cabin at West Point Pleasant on the Jersey shore. Craig joined them for most of the month of October, and then moved back to a New York City hotel. After another month, Meta went back to New York City, and Kemp remained alone to work on his play, *Judas*. A few weeks after Meta left, she wrote Kemp to tell him she had found another lover. It was now his turn to feel devastated; he sympathized with Sinclair.[59] Sinclair, in his unpublished sequel to *Love's Pilgrimage*, "Love's Progress," describes the end of their relationship.[60]

Sinclair sued for divorce with Harry Kemp as correspondent. The only grounds for a divorce in New York State in the early twentieth century were adultery or spousal abuse. Meta agreed not to contest the divorce but the court likely felt there was "collusion" between the parties. The divorce was denied. Sinclair appealed, and it was denied again. Sinclair blamed Catholic judges and a Catholic court. His anger against organized religion appeared in several later works, including *Profits of Religion* (1918). Craig's mother and others warned her to stay away from Sinclair. Although Craig claimed "she lived quietly in New York" and interacted only with George Sterling, this was not the case. Sinclair secretly met with Craig in New York City and probably took Ellen and Craig to the Catskills for a couple of weeks in November.[61]

In February 1912, Sinclair, along with David, departed for Europe to obtain a divorce in Holland. Frederik van Eeden, a Dutch friend, novelist, and poet, had agreed to help him. Under Dutch law, Sinclair could receive a divorce "on the basis of a signed statement by the wife, admitting infidelity."[62] Sinclair needed, however, to establish residency in the Netherlands. He contributed articles to *Physical Culture* magazine on diet and health in various European cultures which brought him needed income. He also interacted with prominent European Socialists.

Craig lived in a New York City apartment and interacted with Meta the winter of 1912. At Sinclair's request, Craig encouraged Meta to send the letter to Sinclair stating she had no objections to the divorce. Unbeknownst to Meta, Craig had been made guardian of David if Sinclair should die. At the beginning of April, Craig visited Ellen Barrows, who was now a secretary to Fisk Warren, a benefactor of Arden, in Harvard, Massachusetts. At this point Craig was secretly engaged to Sinclair.[63]

Sinclair, soon after his arrival in Europe in late February, visited his old friend George Heron in Italy. In early March, he left David at an experimental boarding school in Germany, and from the end of March through April, lived in England. Through the Wilshires he met Lady Russell — known as "Aunt Molly" to her intimate friends — and used her small cottage for writing. Lady Russell had many notable and influential friends. Through her, he met George Bernard Shaw, Frank Harris, reacquainted himself with H.G. Wells, and many others. He worked on *Sylvia*, the story of a Southern Belle, modeled on Craig's childhood stories. Sinclair and his friends devised a plan to get Craig to Europe. In early May, Lady Russell invited Craig to England. Craig's parents agreed to let her go so as to visit art galleries and meet celebrities.

The divorce was finalized May 24, 1912, other than for Meta's letter of approval. Sinclair was given sole custody of David, a decision which would cause problems three years later. In mid–May, David became sick at his German boarding school. Sinclair blamed his illness on the diet at the school, which included cocoa (hot chocolate). He promptly took David back to Holland. Sinclair rented a cottage in Hilversum. Van Eeden thought it safe for Craig to stay at the cottage with Sinclair as "David's governess." In late May, or early June, Craig sailed directly to Holland. Besides residing in Holland, Craig and Sinclair traveled and spend time in Paris.[64]

To avoid anyone knowing their whereabouts, Sinclair arranged for mail from the United States to be sent to the Wilshires, and Craig's mail sent to the Russells, who then forwarded it on. In November 1912, George Sterling asked Craig why he had not heard from her in months. He does not appear to have been aware that she was in Europe. Perhaps she did not disclose her activities as she did not want to risk hurting his feelings by completely breaking off the relationship.[65]

"Experimental Honeymoon," the short story found in the present collection, may have been inspired by Sinclair and Craig's life together in Holland, or Mollie Russell's cottage. The story concerns an aristocratic southern girl who enters a trial marriage with a starving artist. Early "disappointment in love" is also an underlying theme. Craig and Sinclair were both leery of marriage because of disappointment in love. Craig's father had forbidden her to marry the man she loved as he had the reputation of being a heavy drinker and carouser.[66]

Sinclair, Craig, and David, in the early autumn, went to England; David was enrolled at the Highgate boarding school, and Sinclair and Craig lived in Mollie Russell's cottage. At some point Sinclair and Craig decided to marry. In December 1912, Craig returned to the United States when her mother telegraphed her, "I am sick come, Mama." In Mississippi Craig attempted to persuade her father to allow her to marry a divorced man. Sinclair returned to New York to market his new novel, *Sylvia*. "In the interest of propriety, the pair traveled on separate steamers." By doing so, they avoided newspaper reporters looking for gossip. However, a rough December crossing on the *Lusitania*— later sunk by the Germans in World War I — caused Craig to fracture the base of her spine, which caused suffering for years.[67]

Craig's father, a wealthy plantation owner and judge, opposed his daughter's marriage to a divorced socialist muckraker, and refused to attend the event. Her mother and other female relatives, however, approved the marriage, based upon the fact that both families came from the "First Families of Virginia." They even had mutual distant relatives, and both supposedly were descended from a long line of French kings.

Sinclair and Craig were married by an Episcopal priest, April 21, 1913, in Fredericksburg, Virginia. Craig made a good match for Sinclair. Although they were very different personalities, she was happy to be his protégée, let him be in control of their lives, and often reined in his spending. Most importantly for history, she kept and organized his papers over the 48 years of their marriage. However, she freely admitted that she did not love him as she had loved her former fiancé. Marriage to Sinclair may have been an escape from Mississippi into a more exciting world. On the other hand, she did not like David, as he reminded her of Meta. She manipulated Sinclair into sending his son to boarding school or to stay with her parents, and later to have him go to college far from California. Her maneuvers likely caused the estrangement between father and son that lasted until near the end of Upton Sinclair's life.[68]

After their wedding, they collected Craig's younger sister, Dolly, traveled to Europe and picked up David from his school. After travel to France and Germany, they settled for a few weeks in Letchworth, a model village, and then went to London. Sinclair associated with prominent socialists and met Sylvia Pankhurst — a leading woman suffrage combatant — and other women from the British movement. He learned about the cruel treatment suffered by many suffragettes including forced feedings. The experiences of these women are reflected in the three works concerning suffrage in this collection, namely, "Emancipated Husband," "Suffragetteland," and "One Woman's Fight."

Sinclair had seen a performance of a translation of *Les Avariés*, by Eugene Brieux. The play depicts an unfaithful husband who gives his wife, their newborn child, and the child's wet nurse syphilis. Sexually transmitted diseases were not discussed openly in this era, and Sinclair now focused on sexual hygiene along with eugenics as his new crusade. Sexual hygiene was considered an aspect of eugenics — the improvement of the human race.[69] Based upon the drama, Sinclair's novel, *Damaged Goods*, was serialized in Macfadden's *Physical Culture* (June–November 1913) and published in October 1913.

At the end of the summer of 1913, Sinclair and Craig left England and returned to New York. David went back to his English boarding school and Dolly stayed as a paying guest at the Wilshires to attend the Daleroze School of Eurythmics, to study modern dance. The Sinclairs settled briefly in a New York apartment. They moved, December 1913, to Bermuda for six months so he could finish *Sylvia's Marriage*, the sequel to *Sylvia*. In this work Sylvia is infected with gonorrhea and her newborn is blinded by the infection. Sylvia leaves her husband, goes back to the South, and becomes a crusader for sexuality and venereal (sexually transmitted) disease education. When the book was completed, in April 1914, Sinclair and Craig sailed for New York. The book was published in September.

Mary Craig Kimbrough Sinclair in her 1900 graduation photograph.

Within a few weeks of returning to New York, Sinclair learned about the Ludlow Massacre, where women and children had been killed at a Colorado mining camp — a John D. Rockefeller–owned enterprise. Both Sinclair and Craig became involved in silent street demonstrations at the Rockefeller headquarters in New York City. Sinclair was arrested, and the resulting publicity called attention to the conditions at the mines. As a result, Rockefeller recognized the unions and established better working conditions for miners. Sinclair spent a few weeks during the summer in the Colorado mining camps to collect material for a book on the coal industry.

After the Rockefeller incident and other social protest experiences, he assembled material for *The Cry for Justice; An Anthology of Social Protest.* With an advance from the publisher, Sinclair rented a cottage at Croton-on-Hudson. At this artist colony, he met Floyd Dell, his first biographer, along with other artists and writers. Dolly came back from England and became involved in the suffrage movement in New York City. His old theater friends, Margo and Edgar Selwyn, formed a film company and produced *The Jungle.* It was not popular and lost money. In August 1914, when Britain joined France in declaring war on Germany, Sinclair arranged for David to come back to the United States. David was sent to a boarding school in North Carolina. Sinclair remarks in his autobiography, "that left Craig and me free."[70]

In the late spring of 1915, Craig's father, Judge Kimbrough, invited them to stay at Ashton Hall, the family vacation home, in Gulfport, Mississippi. This very large house was occupied only from June through September, the hottest months of the summer. For the rest of the year, Sinclair and Craig could have it for themselves. They accepted the invitation and traveled to Mississippi. Sinclair assembled a tent platform away from the house, near the beach, and began to work on *King Coal*, about the Colorado coal strike of 1913–1914.

Various people came to stay at the house during the summer including, Dolly and David, and Craig's younger brother, Hunter, to keep David company. Meta, too, came to Gulfport and sued for custody of David, who was now thirteen years old. Since Craig's father was a wealthy land owner and a well known Mississippi judge, it would have been difficult for Meta to obtain sole custody of her son. The lawsuit caused further scandal and it was widely reported in the newspapers.

A Catholic judge, who did not believe in divorce, did not grant full custody to Sinclair, either. The court decreed that Meta was allowed to see David at any time when he was in boarding school, and for two weeks at the beginning of summer vacation. She saw little of him due to her own personal circumstances, which included a new marriage and a child.[71] Meta and Sinclair corresponded for several years after the divorce, and she accused him of thwarting the custody agreement. In her autobiography, written in the form of a novel, Meta writes, "It was only after she had signed away the legal custody of her son, that she began to realize that Sinclair had completely repudiated the ideals that had dominated their thoughts for eleven years."[72]

In September 1915, *The Cry for Justice* was published. However, it was overshadowed by the war and the book did not sell well. Besides working on *King Coal*, Sinclair also wrote "An Unmarried Mother." This is the only work included here for which a date and place of residence has been noted on the manuscript.

David spent the winter with the Kimbrough family in Greenwood, Mississippi. In November, Sinclair traveled to southern California without Craig. Craig may not have wanted to leave Mississippi, but her father told her that she "must join her husband" as the family name had already been through too much recent scandal.

Sinclair's subsequent move to California coincided with his waning interest — with a few exceptions — in writing about health topics, Woman suffrage, and the independence of women. At some point, near the end of World War I, he wrote, "Eugenic Celibate Motherhood," a short story in Part III. In the work, Sinclair advocates artificial insemination for unmarried women in order to increase the birth rate, particularly in Australia and England, because so many strong and healthy men had been killed in the war. It is unknown what personal life experiences precipitated this work.

1916 and Beyond: More Social Causes

After Sinclair moved to California, his focus shifted back to the conditions of workers, and corruption found in religion, education, the press, and other industries and organizations. By this time, he was almost forty and finally settled down in one community. The latter part of his life, and his publications, will only be briefly summarized inasmuch as his experiences and personal relationships did not influence the writing of the manuscripts in this book.

In January 1916, Sinclair rented a small house in Coronado, California. Craig joined him the following month. However, they found it too cold and windy. By the end of the year, they bought a house on Sunset Avenue in Pasadena and remained there for 25 years. *King Coal* was rejected by Macmillan, so Sinclair revised it with input from Craig. It was finally published in September of 1917, but did not do well. The *Coal War*, a sequel to *King Coal*, was never published "for world war had come and no one was interested in labor problems anymore."[73] In the first few months in Pasadena, Sinclair met Mrs. Kate Crane-Gartz, a wealthy Pasadena woman, who for many years helped Sinclair fund socialist causes.

David came to stay for the next eighteen months. During his first summer there he worked on the Sinclairs' house to earn money for a car, and the second summer he helped build a swimming pool. At the end of the summer vacation, he went to high school in Greenwood, Mississippi. In the meantime, Craig began to invest in real estate. She bought and sold lots and fixed up houses for a number of years as a way of earning money.[74]

Sinclair did not agree with the socialists' pacifist stand on the war. Therefore, on July 22, 1917, he resigned from the American Socialist Party. This action closed socialist publications to his writings. In order to publish his material, Sinclair started "a little socialist magazine to support the American position in the world war." This magazine, *Upton Sinclair's*, was printed between April 1918 and February 1919. He ran it out of his house, and it was supported by Mrs. Gartz. However, the magazine did not prosper and merged with *Appeal to Reason*, which later became *Haldeman-Julius Weekly*, named after the new owner. With the merger, Sinclair had one full page for a column called "Upton Sinclair's" where he discussed many topics.[75]

Near the end of the war years, he wrote two war-related novels. *Jimmie Higgins* (1919) is the story of a socialist patriot who went to war but suffers conflicting feelings — much like Sinclair. *100% American* is a companion-piece. In this work, a young American fights against the "Red Terror." Sinclair self-published it in 1920.

Sinclair now turned his attention to further "muckraking," and exposed corruption in numerous organizations. Many of these exposés he published himself, as no mainstream publisher would touch them. Most included examples from his own experiences. The first institution he criticized was religion. He announced, in *The Profits of Religion,* that it was the first of a series of social critiques of various organizations or industries. *Profits* contains a number of essays about different religious sects, and describes them as money making entities for their leaders. It was originally serialized in his newsletter, *Upton Sinclair's*, and published by him in book form in October 1918. Sinclair wrote another book on Christianity and socialism, *They Call Me Carpenter* (1922) in which Christ is a carpenter in southern California. His last days are described with contemporary characters playing the roles of the biblical personalities. Christ is condemned as a "Red" — communist — by the masses for repeating words right out of the Bible.

Sinclair self-published the next three works in the series. *The Brass Check* (1920) explores the newspaper industry. The book describes Sinclair's own battles with reporters, editors, and publishers; and it sold well. Corruption in higher education was exposed in *The Goose-Step* (1923). Sinclair toured various university campuses around the country to collect data. He relates his own experiences at Columbia, describes the influence of big business over the university, and attacks college athletics for being too commercial. Secondary education, in *The Goslings* (1924), was the target of his next exposé. He examines the pressure on teachers that prevents them from discussing certain topics, and how school boards are bought. In these publications, Sinclair recommended unions for workers in white collar industries.

After being jailed for reading the Constitution of the United States out loud on private property, and helping to found the Southern California chapter of the ACLU (American Civil Liberties Union), Sinclair wrote a comedy, *The Singing Jailbirds*, which he self-published in 1924. It received positive reviews in New York.

Sinclair corresponded with readers who turned to him for guidance with health and personal matters after reading his writings in *Appeal to Reason*. In September 1921, based upon this correspondence, the Macmillan Company published *The Book of Life: Mind and Body*. A second volume — *Love and Society* — was printed in 1922. The two volumes were combined together and published immediately by the Haldeman-Julius Company, which printed many of Sinclair's later books. Topics covered in these two volumes ranged from cures to birth control.

In the post–World War I years, southern California was in the midst of an oil boom. Craig owned property that lay in the oil field, and exchanged it for a cottage on the beach in Alamitos Bay. They moved from Pasadena and lived in the cottage for a few years. Based upon the corruption he observed in the grab for oil-rich land, Sinclair wrote *Oil!* (1927).[76] The novel, a best seller, became Sinclair's second most known work. In this book, he details the lives of impoverished oil workers, small lot owners, and greedy capitalists. The book was banned in Boston because Sinclair had mentioned birth control. Angry at the city's action, he traveled to Boston with a "fig-leaf edition" of the book — the offending pages were replaced by a drawing of a fig leaf— and sold it on the streets. This activity, of course, increased interest in the work and boosted sales.

During his stay in Boston in the summer of 1927, Sinclair interviewed Bartolomeo Vanzetti. Vanzetti and Nicola Sacco had been found guilty of a crime they probably did not commit and were executed. Sinclair went back to Boston and gathered further material for a two volume book about their case. In the fall of 1927, he began writing *Boston*. This two-volume book was published in November 1928. It portrays discrimination against Italian workers, and a grave miscarriage of justice.

Craig began to practice Christian Science, in the mid–1920s, for relief of pain she had suffered for a number of years. This led her to study mental healing and psychic phenomena. Around 1928, at the beach house, Craig began to experiment with mental telegraphy. Sinclair wrote *Mental Radio* (1930), based upon the results of her psychic experiments.[77]

Over the decade of the 1930s, Sinclair wrote a wide variety of works influenced by events he and Craig had experienced. Three close friends of Sinclair and Craig committed suicide as the result of alcoholism. These included George Sterling (1869–1926), Craig's former fiancé, "Jerry Calhoun" (his true name is unknown), and a decade before, Jack London (1876–1916). Their deaths, along with Sinclair's experiences as a youth with his alcoholic father, led to the novel *The Wet Parade*, published in September 1931. The work supported the continuation of Prohibition. A few years after Floyd Dell's biography of Sinclair was published, Sinclair came out with his autobiography, *American Outpost* (1932).

Sinclair was the first celebrity to run for governor of California. During 1933–1934, he ran as a Democrat on the "EPIC platform"— End Poverty in California. He wrote two campaign propaganda books. In October 1933, *I, Governor of California and How I Ended Poverty* was published, and *I, Candidate for Governor, and How I Got Licked*, was released after he lost the election, in January of 1935.

Sinclair was known around the world and his books had been translated into numerous languages. He was a finalist, in 1932, for the Nobel Prize in Literature, although he did not win the award. In 1933, he invested in the production of a film, *Thunder over Mexico*, with Sergei Eisenstein, the famous Russian filmmaker. This was a mistake. For weeks Craig attempted to get him to abandon the project, and he lost much money on the venture. Sinclair had met Henry Ford in California, and self published *The Flivver King* (1937) about Ford and the Ford Motor Company. The book was widely read. His favorite work during the 1930s was *Our Lady* (1939), a novelette of what would happen if Jesus' mother, Mary, was transported into 1930s Los Angeles.

As World War II approached, Sinclair began a historical fiction series about war throughout the first half of the twentieth century. These novels were popular during the 1940s. His protagonist, Lanny Budd, was the illegitimate son of a "munitions making father." Over the years, Budd associates with notable people and is a player in complex situations in various wars and political intrigues. Sinclair wrote eleven novels in this series in thirteen years. In the first book, *World's End* (1940), Budd becomes a witness to the formation of League of Nations after World War I. *Dragon's Teeth* (1942), the third book in the series, won Sinclair the 1943 Pulitzer Prize for literature. This work chronicles the rise of German Nazism. The last book, *The Return of Lanny Budd* (1953), is a Cold War McCarthy-era adventure.

At the onset of World War II, Craig feared a possible invasion or attack by the Japanese because southern California was a major shipping center. Therefore, in 1942, they bought a neo–Mediterranean villa on Myrtle Avenue, in Monrovia, California, which was located in the relatively isolated San Gabriel Valley. The well constructed house provided safety for the vast collection of Sinclair's papers. Concrete storage areas were also built for the collection. Sinclair did much of his later writing in Monrovia, although he did temporarily reside in other communities.[78]

In 1956 Sinclair wrote a semi-autobiographical book about "social drinking" in the United States. It documents the ruin of many gifted individuals — many of them his friends — due to alcoholism. *Cup of Fury* became one of his best-selling works.

Craig increasingly became a "hypochondrial hermit" and retreated from outside contact. Arthur remarks, "Craig's insistence on privacy was such that Western Union had to deliver its telegrams to Sinclair by throwing them over his locked gate because his wife refused to answer the doorbell or telephone." Sinclair's social life became increasingly restricted.[79] They also played hide-and-seek with Mrs. Gartz by moving from one place to another. Gartz had become a Communist and Sinclair was not interested in contact with her or her Red friends anymore.

By 1954, southern California had changed and Craig was sick. They moved to the small town of Buckeye, near Phoenix, Arizona, not far from her brother, Hunter. Shortly after moving, Craig began to experience congestive heart failure, and perhaps had a heart attack. They soon moved back to California where Sinclair nursed her though the final years of her life. In 1957, the Lilly Library at Indiana University completed a deal to acquire all of Sinclair's papers. In 1959, Craig published her autobiography, *Southern Belle*. However, it was likely written by Sinclair, with Craig's input, as Craig was weak and dying.

During the 1960s came the final chapter of Sinclair's life. Until a few years before his death, Sinclair still wrote, and published two autobiographical works. *My Lifetime in Letters* (1960) is a collection of correspondence with many notable individuals. He added material from the later part of his life to *American Outpost* (1932), his initial autobiography. It was published as *The Autobiography of Upton Sinclair* (1962).

Craig died April 26, 1961, and her ashes were shipped to a brother in Greenwood, Mississippi, to be interred in the family plot. Within six months of her death, Sinclair married Mary "May" Elizabeth Willis, a widow from Claremont, California. Meta, now in poor health, was living in St. Petersburg, Florida, with her third husband, John Stone. Sinclair resumed contact with his former wife after sending her a copy of his autobiography. He corresponded with her husband, but not directly with her. Meta died October 3, 1964. After her death, her papers were added to the Lilly Library collection.[80]

In 1967, Sinclair and May went to live in an apartment in Rockville, Maryland, near one of her daughters. David, now a prominent physicist, and his second wife lived in Martinville, New Jersey. Father and son had reconciled. May died December 18, 1967, and Sinclair died, a little less than a year later, November 25, 1968, at age ninety in a nursing home. He was buried beside May in the Rock Creek Cemetery, Washington, DC.

Personal experiences, family members, and close friends often color a person's attitudes and behaviors. Sinclair's writings on relationships and dietary obsessions, in particular during the period of 1900 through 1915, were largely influenced by the breakdown of his health and the mismatched relationship with his first wife, Meta. These influences and experiences are seen in the short essays, sketches, and stories in this book. Yet, the complete legacy of Upton Sinclair, one of the most influential American novelists in terms of social reform, still remains to be fully explored in the Lilly Library collection at Indiana University in Bloomington, Indiana.

Notes

This short biography heavily draws upon the *Autobiography of Upton Sinclair*. For certain time periods, it utilizes *Thyrsis and Corydon*, the unpublished autobiography of Sinclair's first wife, Meta, and *Southern Belle*, the autobiography of his second wife, Craig. Sinclair's autobiographical novel, *Love's Pilgrimage*, and Harry Kemp's *Tramping on Life* are also used to a minor extent in addition to the Sinclair and related manuscripts at the Lilly Library.

ABBREVIATIONS OF SOURCES

AUS	*Autobiography of Upton Sinclair* (1962).
LP	*Love's Pilgrimage* (Upton Sinclair, 1911).
SB	*Southern Belle* (Mary Craig Kimbrough Sinclair, 1957).
Sinclair mss.	Sinclair manuscripts, Lilly Library Manuscripts Collection, Indiana University, Bloomington, Indiana.
Sinclair, MCK	Sinclair, MCK, manuscripts, Lilly Library Manuscripts Collection, Indiana University, Bloomington, Indiana.
Stone mss.	Stone Manuscripts. Lilly Library Manuscripts collection, Indiana University, Bloomington, Indiana (The Stone manuscripts contain the correspondence, clippings, and papers of Sinclair's first wife, Meta Fuller).
T&C	*Thyrsis and Corydon*. Folders III–V. Keen, Meta Fuller, Stone Manuscripts. Lilly Library Manuscripts Collection, Indiana University, Bloomington, Indiana.
TOL	*Tramping on Life* (Kemp, Harry; 1922).

CITATIONS

1. *AUS*, 6–7, 16; *LP*, 3.
2. *AUS*, 8.
3. Meta was born in San Francisco, California, February 7, 1880.
4. *AUS*, 8.
5. *AUS*, 9.
6. *AUS*, 21.
7. *AUS*, 25.
8. *AUS*, 34–35, 49–51; *LP*, 2.
9. *AUS*, 52.
10. His Uncle Bland. *AUS*, 78.
11. LP, 50. Sinclair throughout his writings idealizes the woman who is independent and defies convention. However, Meta continuously writes that he will not let her be independent and wants to control all aspects of her life.

12. *AUS*, 80. In his later writings, based upon his experiences, he champions legalizing dissemination of birth control information.

13. *T&C*, Folder, III, Part II, 6; *T&C*, Folder V, 6; *LP*, 111–112. The mention of David being born at "an inopportune time" in many writings suggests that he was unwanted. This is manifested by Sinclair sending David off to boarding school or away from where Sinclair was living, primarily after his divorce and subsequent marriage to Craig.

14. *AUS*, 80; *LP*, 114–115. In Sinclair's later writings, he opposes abortion but supports the use of birth control to prevent unwanted pregnancy. This is found in "Experimental Honeymoon."

15. *AUS*, 83, 91.

16. Sinclair, "Perfect Health," *Contemporary Review* (January–June:1910), 431.

17. *Ibid.*; *AUS*, 87. Later in his memoirs he realized that, he in fact, was a health fanatic. Evidence of this abounds throughout many of his works.

18. See Mattson, *Upton Sinclair* (2006), 45, for more detail concerning Sinclair's socialist philosophy which was woven through most of his writings for several decades.

19. *AUS*, 95; *T&C*, Folder V, 2–3. During this time, Meta expresses much frustration with child rearing and isolation from others.

20. *T&C*, Folder V, 6, 13, 37.

21. *AUS*, 97. Meta does not mention this incident in her manuscripts.

22. This engagement was the first major land battle of the Civil War.

23. *AUS*, 106–107. This is the first time that Meta's father appears to have shown some acceptance of him.

24. *T&C*, Folder V, 6; *LP*, 147–147. Meta mentions chronic "womb troubles" which she blames on walking up and down stairs postpartum, during recovery from childbirth. The unknown illness could have been a miscarriage, undiagnosed appendicitis, an abortion, or surgery for a tumor.

25. *AUS*, 123.

26. See Ahouse, *Upton Sinclair* (1994) and Gottesman, *Upton Sinclair* (1973) for details concerning most of Sinclair's books and manuscripts.

27. *T&C*, Folder V, 8. It is interesting to note that Craig in the 1920s also engaged in mental healing and Christian Science for her various health problems.

28. *T&C*, Folder V, 10. The status of the extra-marital affairs of both Meta and Sinclair are unclear. Sinclair claims his affairs were "intellectual," and Meta claims hers were "emotional" until near the end of their marriage when they both admit to several sexual liaisons.

29. *T&C*, Folder V, 15; *San Francisco Examiner*, January 30, 1909. In this issue Sinclair expresses his opinions concerning trial marriage.

30. *T&C*, Folder V, 16; *AUS*, 130.

31. *AUS*, 135. Because the community was in financial trouble, some even accused him of burning it down to collect the insurance money.

32. *T&C*, Folder V, 19.

33. Sinclair, Upton, "Perfect Health," *Contemporary Review* (January–June 1910), 438.

34. *AUS*, 137–138; *T&C*, Folder V, 19–20; Sinclair, "Perfect Health," 438. Inasmuch as "appendicitis" was often used as a cover for an abortion, she may have devel-

oped this life-threatening infection as a result of an abortion and not misdiagnosed appendicitis. Antibiotics were not available until the early 1940s, and the death rate was high from peritonitis.

35. *AUS*, 138.

36. *T&C*, Folder V, 19.

37. See Sinclair to J. H. Kellogg, July 20, 1910. Sinclair Mss. Series I. Note: John Harvey Kellogg, M.D., ran the Battle Creek Sanitarium. His younger brother, W. K. Kellogg, owned the cereal company. Details concerning the two brothers and health fanaticism during this era are found in Engs, *The Progressive Era's Health Reform Movement* (2005).

38. It was rewritten as a novel and serialized in *Appeal to Reason* in 1914, before being published in book form in 1924 by Haldeman-Julius.

39. See Engs, *The Progressive Era's Health Reform Movement* (2005).

40. *AUS*, 145; *T&C*, Folder V, 23–24.

41. *AUS*, 146.

42. *AUS*, 150–151.

43. *T&C*, Folder V, 24.

44. *T&C*, Folder V, 31, 36, 38.

45. See Harris, *Upton Sinclair* (1975), 125; Scott, *Upton Sinclair* (1997), 110.

46. The close friendship between Craig and Meta is documented in the writings, correspondence, and publications of Sinclair, Meta, and Harry Kemp.

47. *T&C*, Folder V, 31–33, 36; Kuttner to Meta, April 6, 1910, Folder 1910, Stone mss.

48. *T&C*, Folder V, 40.

49. Meta to David Sinclair, February 18, 1942, Folder 1912–1965, Stone mss.

50. *T&C*, Folder V, 39–42.

51. Inspection of correspondence, autobiographies, and autobiographical novels of Sinclair, Meta, Craig, and Kemp, and weekly correspondence from Sterling to Craig show conflicting stories from late 1910 through the autumn of 1912. Both Meta and Sinclair remark that Meta went to Gulfport, Mississippi, in the winter of 1910 at the invitation of Craig (*T&C*, Folder V, 42–43; *AUS*, 166–167). Craig in her autobiography implies she went up north in the fall of 1910 to get advice about her book and remained there. She met Sinclair to discuss her book "late in the season" (*SB*, 68; 77). Sinclair remarks that Craig invited him to New York in April (*AUS*, 173).

52. Correspondence between Sinclair and Meta suggest that Meta — and Craig with her — returned to New York in June 1911 (Sinclair to Meta, in Gulfport, June 5, 1911, Folder 1911, Stone mss.). Meta claims she went back up north alone and Craig soon followed (*T&C*, 44–45).

53. *T&C*, Folder V, 44–45.

54. Neither Sinclair nor Craig, in their autobiographies, mention that Craig spent time and lived with Meta during this traumatic time. Both Meta and Kemp relate that the two women were together in New York City, and also on the Jersey shore (see *T&C*, Folder V, 51–52; *TOL*, 402–403). George Sterling also verifies this in his correspondence (see Sterling to MC Sinclair. Folders 1911, 1912, Sinclair, MCK, mss.).

55. *T&C*, Folder V, 48; *TOL*, 394, 403–405; *AUS*, 174. "Sinclair to Sue in Arden," *New York Times*, August 25, 1911. *ProQuest Historical Newspapers*. Downloaded: 27 February 2008. <http://www.proquest.com/>

56. *T&C*, Folder V, 54; *TOL*, 405; *AUS*, 175.

57. *T&C*, Folder V, p. 56–59; "Use Endearing Terms While Talking Divorce." *Los Angeles Times,* August 29, 1911. "Sinclair Now Shuns Publicity." *New York Times,* August 30, 1911. *ProQuest Historical Newspapers.* Downloaded: 27 February 2008. <http://www.proquest.com/>

58. *AUS,* 175; *TOL,* 412. *Brass Check,* 105–107.

59. *TOL,* 415, 433–434, 438.

60. "Love's Progress" is found in the Lilly Library manuscript collection. Meta, for several more years, searched for a "soul mate." *The Washington Post,* June 18, 1913, reports that Meta was engaged to be married to a Herbert Halliwell of Poughkeepsie, New York, son of a prominent jeweler. The same newspaper, June 30, 1915, reports that Meta was named as correspondent in a divorce suit of William Roaul, a prominent Atlanta, Georgia, socialist. Meta married Lester Keen, a businessman, in New York City on January 9, 1916; they had one son. They moved to Florida in the early 1930s. Six months after Keen's death, she married John A. Stone, August 18, 1947.

61. Other than for a few days in August and a few days in mid–September, Sterling spent his time in Sag Harbor, New York. He returned around September 23, 1911 to California. (See Sterling to MCSinclair. Folder 1911, Sinclair, MCK, mss.) In a letter to Craig, October 9, 1911, Sinclair recommends that she use his mother's address to receive mail in order to deceive her parents and others as to her whereabouts. Sterling sent letters to Craig at this address in November 1911.

62. *AUS,* 177. Meta agreed to do this.

63. On May 2, 1912, Lady Russell invites Craig to come to England. As to detailed arrangements between Sinclair and Craig and others, see Sinclair to Craig, May 22, 1912, Folder 1912, Series VI, Sinclair mss.

64. In her book, Craig remarks that she "accidentally" met Sinclair in England at the Wilshires'. Sinclair in his autobiography says he went to England to meet Craig so as to "collect local color for his new novel, Sylvia" (*AUS,* 180). However, there is no evidence for either of these stories. Russell in a letter to Sinclair, October 10, 1912, states, "I hope M.C. [Mary Craig] will like me" which suggests Russell did not meet Craig until after she had been in Europe for four months.

Leon Harris, an earlier biographer, suggests Sinclair and Craig lived and traveled together as a married couple in Europe (Harris, 140). Several letters in the Sinclair mss. collection confirm they were together throughout this time. Anthony Arthur, a recent biographer, based upon Harris's interview with Craig's younger sister, Dolly, argues that Craig went to England in March 1912 to obtain an abortion which Mary Wilshire arranged for her. The invite from Lady Russell was a cover-up (Arthur, *Radical Innocent* [2006], 144–145; Harris, Upton Sinclair, 126, note 374). There is no evidence that Craig was in Europe before the beginning of June 1912, which would have been too late for a first-trimester abortion. If Craig had obtained an abortion, it would have been in the fall of 1912, or perhaps the summer of 1913 after they were married. See Folder 1912, Series IV, Sinclair mss., and Folder 1912, July–December, correspondence, Sinclair mss.

65. See Sterling to MC Sinclair, Folder 1912, Sinclair, MCK, mss.

66. *SB,* 50–51.

67. *AUS,* 186. Cable from Mrs. Kimbrough to Craig, December 6, 1912, Folder 1912, July–December, Sinclair mss.

68. *SB*, 384; *AUS*, 191; Harris, 143.

69. See Engs, *The Eugenics Movement* (2005) for the connections between the crusades, and their crusaders, for birth control, sex education, venereal disease education and prevention, Prohibition, diet and exercise, and eugenics. All these health campaigns were for the improvement of the human race, "a perfect child," "better baby," or eugenics.

70. *AUS*, 204. This statement gives some insight into Sinclair's and Craig's feelings toward the upbringing of David.

71. Sinclair in his autobiography mentions that he has custody for six months of the year (*AUS*, 210). Documents concerning the result of the court degree suggest this is not accurate. (See letter from Meta to Lester Keen, July 31, 1915, Folder 1912–1965, Stone mss.)

72. Meta to Sinclair, May 25, 1917, Stone mss.; *T&C*, Folder V, 65.

73. *AUS*, 217.

74. *SB*, 210, 214, 221, 234–235.

75. *AUS*, 218, 221; *SB*, 240–245, 252.

76. *SB*, 301, 304.

77. *SB*, 304, 507, 319–320; *AUS*, 244–247.

78. *AUS*, 303–304; National Historic Landmarks, Upton Sinclair House. http://tps.cr.nps.gov/nhl/detail.cfm?ResourceId=1076&ResourceType=Building. Downloaded: February 21, 2008.

79. Arthur, 145.

80. John Stone to Sinclair, March 3, 1965, Folder 1912–1965, Stone mss.

PART I

Woman Suffrage and Emancipation

I believe that women ought to earn their own livings, and be independent and free from any man's control. — Upton Sinclair, *Sylvia's Marriage*, 1914

CHAPTER ONE

Suffragetteland

Editor's note: Sinclair, in this short sketch for a comedy, satirizes militant woman suffrage crusaders. He speculates on what might happen if they became completely independent of men, and then a man suddenly comes into their midst. Sinclair did, however, support the concept of women's rights, decried sexual naïveté among women, and championed sex education for both men and women, as seen in several of his publications (see Sylvia's Marriage [1913] *in particular). Only one copy of the two page draft for this proposed script was found. It was written around 1912-1913 when he interacted with British suffragettes while in Britain. Women in the United States received voting rights equal to men upon the ratification of the Nineteenth Amendment to the Constitution on August 18, 1920. Women in Britain did not receive suffrage rights equal to men until 1925.*

The essence of this comedy is: An island inhabited by fifty women, and only one man. What happens?

Suffrage headquarters on Fifth Avenue. Congress has passed a bill giving the vote to women; but word comes that the Supreme Court has declared it unconstitutional. Some of the radicals, in a rage, declare that they will secede to Suffragetteland, and govern themselves, with all the votes they want. A woman doctor makes the portentous announcement that she has solved the problem of the manless infant. So at last women can be independent, there can be a manless world.

Suffragetteland is an island in the South Seas, to which the British government has been exiling the militants. Warships steam about, and no human being is ever allowed upon its shores. The women govern themselves. The American women who wish to join them go to London. Scene showing them smashing pictures in the National Gallery. One young American doctor

---

"Suffragetteland," Sinclair Manuscripts, Series III, Writings, Articles, Lilly Library, Indiana University, Bloomington, IN.

43

has followed his wife, and prevents her from using her hatchet, and so she is not arrested; in a rage she vows that she will never see him again.

Scenes on Suffragetteland. The women vote. A kind of idyllic, outdoor life, pretty costumes, etc. A procession of nurses, bearing the new manless infants. But the women are bored. For some reason, life lacks its spice.

There is a storm at sea, and a man is washed ashore, clinging to a spar. It is the young American doctor. In despair at having been deserted by his wife, he has shipped as doctor on a supply ship of the British fleet, and he is now the sole survivor of a wreck. He is on the island, and there is no way to get him off.

The comedy possibilities are as endless as the complications between the sexes. Immediately some woman is found powdering her nose. She is sent to prison; but others resort to other arts. The doctor is a virtuous married man; but he is handsome; and the women are not to be withstood. (They have no excuse for wanting him, but they want him). The doctor is seduced, kidnapped, cajoled; he becomes the centre of insurrections and civil wars. Some women take to gorgeous costumes; others to celibacy and hair-shirts. Some preachers of Puritanism are arrested and put in jail, where they at once begin to hunger-strike and have to be forcibly fed. The turmoil is ended by the doctor asserting his male supremacy, putting down all rebellion with a firm hand, and making himself king. Two years later we see him as an oriental despot, seated on a throne being fanned with peacock fans and served by armies of adoring slaves.

At the climax of some oriental scene, the sound of cannon heard, warships approaching in the offing. Intense excitement. Signals make known that the U.S. has granted suffrage, and the women have gone to war with England, and destroyed the British fleet, so as to free the martyrs on Suffragetteland. A procession of votes with banners come in, with music, etc. The women are in a panic. At all hazards they must hide the dreadful truth as to what has happened to them. They dress up the young doctor as a woman. Enter a suffrage parade of women in full regalia, speeches, etc. In the midst of this [the wife] of the young doctor recognizes him under his disguise. She rushes to him; she has her suspicions as to the manless infants.

CHAPTER TWO

One Woman's Fight

Editor's note: This short work of fiction, which may have been based on a true story of one woman, or at least a composition of women, is a dark tale in contrast to the two comedies concerning women's rights, "Suffragetteland" and "The Emancipated Husband." The action of the story takes place in Britain. An upper-middle-class young woman finds she has been kept totally ignorant of the meaning of marriage and sex until it is explained by a young female medical student. This topic is not acceptable to her parents, and because she refuses to cease her friendship with the student, she is kept prisoner by her family, from whom she escapes. She is disinherited, takes up the suffrage cause, and becomes a militant, to the detriment of her health and life. Two copies of the twelve-page draft for this work were found. It was probably written during 1912-1913, when Sinclair interacted with British woman suffrage leaders during his two trips to England.

ONE WOMAN'S FIGHT

A True Story.   By Upton Sinclair

"I can't understand how women of refinement can do such things!" exclaimed one of the ladies at the evening gathering. She had picked up from the table, a magazine, with some pictures of an English suffragette, struggling in the arms of a policeman. "I could believe such behavior of street women, but for ladies, people who come from decent homes, and have had education!"

Then another woman spoke: "I have heard that remark a hundred times; and each time I make the same answer, I will explain it to you — some day when you can give me time to tell you a story. It is a story of what happened to one woman in England, and it sums up for me the whole

---

"One Woman's Fight: A True Story," Sinclair Manuscripts, Series III, Writings, Articles, Lilly Library, Indiana University, Bloomington, IN.

meaning of the militant movement. It has never failed to throw new light on the question for those who heard it."

"Tell it now," said one of the company.

"No," was the reply. "It would take to long, and one person should not talk so much in company." But others urged her, and so at last she said, "Very well."

The above is a real conversation; and the story is a true story. It might have cast it into fictional form, but as its truth is a part of interest, I have thought it best to write it just as I heard it.

I am, as you know, a doctor. But when this happened I was a student, and had gone to England on a summer visit. An aunt of mine, who lives abroad a great deal, happened to know intimately an English family, to which she gave me an introduction. The head of the family was a clergy-man of the Church of England, the rector of an important church in a large city; and my aunt explained to me that he was a man of strict ideas, and that I must be careful not to reveal to this family any notions which they might consider improper for a young woman of refinement to hold. I would be, she said, an object of some suspicion, as a woman medical student was a thing of which they had no previous experience. But they would take me in for her sake, and they were personally such lovable and charming people, that it would be well worth my while to mind my ps and qs, and make myself agreeable to them.

So when I wrote that I was in England, I received a cordial invitation to visit them. I wrote at a happy time, said the clergyman's letter. Their youngest daughter was about to enter the blessed state of matrimony. I could not help smiling, as I read this, for my aunt had told me that there were five unmarried daughters, the eldest of them on the way beyond thirty, and so I could imagine that a wedding would be a not unacceptable event to that household. I replied, explaining that my engagements made it impossible for me to get to the ceremony, but that I could come two or three days afterwards, if it was agreeable.

So I got there just after the excitement — in time to finish up the baked meats and the cake from the wedding. I never saw the bride, but I was shown her picture — a typical English girl, with a fresh complexion, regular features, and clear candid eyes gazing straight out of the picture at you. She was about twenty-two, I judged; and the groom, whose picture I saw also, was a man whose hair was very evidently thin on top. He was also a typical English person, a country gentleman with considerable estates; he looked to be a hearty liver, who would need to ride to hounds a great deal to keep his waist-line within limits. I set some store by my judgment of faces, and I distrusted the man's, and I thought at once: "I wonder how he ever won that girl!"

I got along very well with the family. I said nothing about my medical propensities, and I suppose they made allowances for other things because of my being an American. When they found that I came from Iowa, they were perfectly prepared to hear accounts of Indians and wolves and buffalo. But when the father found that I went to church and followed the service acceptably, and had been to a Shakespeare festival and could recite long passages from the plays, he thawed out entirely, and was willing to let me play tennis with the girls.

I struck up a friendship with one of them — Mary, the youngest of those that were left. She was only a year older than Hannah, the bride, and three years younger than the next sister, and so she had been Hannah's playmate and chum, and told me about her, — what a lovely girl she was, and how the wedding had gone, and no end of girl-gossip. But I noticed that she did not say much about the groom, as I soon divined that she did not like him, in spite of her conviction that it would be presumptuous of her to have any ideas concerning her sister's marriage, contrary to those of her father and mother.

I was a wonderful person to Mary; a woman who meant to have a career of my own, to go out and face the world without the aid of a man. I was already doing something quite unheard of to this sheltered girl, who could not quite conceive how a woman with delicacy of feeling could study the things that doctors had to deal with. I saw that she shrank back timidly when I ventured to refer however vaguely to medical matters. She liked me, as a woman — she soon came to love me; but as a medical student I was something portentous to her.

She was no less interesting to me than I to her. The girls I had known were the free, independent daughters of the West; this sheltered, home-bound dreamer was like a captive in a cage to me. She was young, full of yearning, of vaguely-felt desires; but the round of her life was tennis, tea-parties, church societies and sewing classes, and the timid, soulful courtesies of her father's tame curate. She was restless, yet so utterly ignorant of life that she had no idea why — no idea that it was possible that a clergyman's daughter could have anything more in life than she had. And when, slow and cautiously, I began to hint at wider possibilities for women, she would gaze at me with the startled look of a deer that hesitates before running. She had dark, wistful eyes, and a sensitive face; and I could see her quivering with interest and curiosity, that made her come back to me again and again to ask more questions about America, about all the new ideas of which she got hints from me.

All this in three or four days — and then came the crash. Something had happened to Hannah, we could not tell what, but there had come a telegram from France to the father, and he had packed his bag and rushed off to a train. The mother was tearful and terrified, the girls were silent and bewildered, and there was a general atmosphere of dread about the house. I thought that I ought to go, but Mary clung to me — some instinct seemed to tell her that she would need new guidance in this emergency. On her account I stayed on.

In four days the father came back — looking ten years older. He said nothing to me directly — in fact I only saw him for a few moments. But from the girls and the maid and one or two friends, I picked up some hints of the story. Three days after her marriage, the young bride was a raving lunatic, and the poor father had had to go — the groom having shirked the task — to have her brought to her own country, and put in a private asylum.

As a medical student, I had some idea of what this meant. But I knew still more about it because of my familiarity with the literature of feminism. It was of course impossible to talk plainly to any one in the household about the matter, but from a relative of the family who came in I got a few hints which made me certain that my suspicion was correct. The bridegroom was a man who had had considerable of a past. He was known among his companions as a man of domineering temper — it was a man who told me this, and he described how he had once seen the party in question strike and employee with his whip. The girl had not loved him. The match had been made by the parents, and the social position and family prestige of the man had been their principle consideration. These few things I put together, and then I watched the daughters of this household who were like people struck dumb with terror. I felt certain that they had no remotest idea of what it all meant. Perhaps I had no business to tell them, — I did not intend to tell them; it seemed to happen of itself.

Mary came into my room in the small hours of the morning; she had been pacing the floor until she was exhausted. Sleep was out of the question for her, so she fled to me. I caught her to my arms and tried to comfort her. We sat on the side or the bed and suddenly she turned upon me staring at my eyes. "What do you suppose that we have done," she exclaimed "that God should have sent such a thing to us."

And how could I fail to answer such a question. "My dear," I said, "I feel quite sure that God had nothing whatever to do with it, and it is sheer blasphemy to attempt to put it all upon him."

From the way she looked at me, I saw that she did not in the least understand, so I added, "It is man that is responsible, you may be sure."

She was sitting string at me. "What to you mean by that?" she asked.

I hesitated, wondering if I had said too much, but she clung to me with convulsive fingers. "How can man be responsible for such things?"

"One man is responsible," I said, and then in the silence I thought, and added, "No, perhaps two, your father also."

"My father!" she cried, more bewildered than ever. "What do you mean?"

Still I hesitated.

"What can you know about it? Tell me, tell me, I must know about it, I must understand."

"Mary dear," I said, "I have studied these questions. I know more about them than most young women, but I don't know if you would thank me for telling you. I am sure that your parents do not intend that you shall be told."

"Mary, Mary," she cried, her voice falling away to a horrified whisper. "You mean that my mother and father know what it means?"

"I don't know about your mother," I said, "I am quite sure that your father does."

"But how can you know? You know nothing about it."

"I know the circumstances under which your sister married, and know what sometimes happens. The medical books are full of such cases."

"What do you mean," cried the girl. "What can have happened, to cause this horrible thing?"

"Your sister," I said, "has married a man she does not love. She was ignorant, I do not doubt. She did not know what marriage meant, and he perhaps did not realize the depth of her ignorance, the need of gentleness

49

and patience in telling her." I stopped, supposing that I had said enough. But the look of blank consternation remained on the girl's face.

"What in the world do you mean," she cried "What is there about marriage that could drive my sister mad?"

So, little by little, I came to realize the depths of this young woman's ignorance. Many people refuse to believe that it is possible for women to come to maturity without knowing the meaning of their sex life, but in every company of women you will find cases of the same sort if you inquire. Particularly with city bred women, who are far removed from Nature and never have these things forced upon their attention. This girl had no remotest idea of the meaning of marriage, no more ideas than a child in arms. I have met many girls who knew that they did not know, who had been deliberately taught that they must not know, that they must avoid all mention of the subject and all thinking about it. But this girl did not even know that she was ignorant, did not even know that there was any-thing for her to know. And if a volcano had opened up beneath her feet, she could not have been more astonished and more horrified when I pro-ceeded, as gently and simply as I could, to explain to her what marriage meant, and how it came about that women had children.

And I had to explain not merely the normal things of sex, but the abnormal. The passions of the brutal and licentious man who had never learned self-restraint and who had turned over to his mercy or lack of it an innocent and trusting girl.

When I tell this story, people say that it is an abnormal case, that such things surely cannot happen very often. I refer them to the medical books — there is not a physician who has not come upon many such cases in the course or his lifetime, and every specialist in the mental disorders of women knows that a quite definite percentage of hysterias and sexual aberrations are caused by the nervous shock which women receive upon their bridal night.

All this I told to Mary, and at last she understood why I considered that her sister's tragedy was to be blamed upon man's stupidity and not upon the malevolence of God. I thought that this girl too would go out of her mind with horror of the revelation. She paced up and down the room, she clung to me sobbing and moaning. New aspects of the horror would suddenly be revealed to her. How much she understood that had been dark to her before. She had hated and feared the man, she had not wanted her sister to marry him, but had not dared to say so. She knew that her sister would never have married him if she had know the truth, and Oh! the folly and the blindness of her parents. "They should have told her, they should have told her," she wept again and again. "They should have told all of us."

"Don't any of you know?" I asked, "Your sisters, as old as they are?"

"Of course they don't know," cried Mary. "How could they know? Who would tell them?"

"It seems incredible to me —." I began.

"I don't believe that any girls know," cried the other, "at least, none of my friends, girls of my sort."

Well, I don't want to make this story too long. I tried to comfort her, and I told her that we would at least make this much out of the tragedy; we would teach her and her sisters. I promised her that I would talk to the latter myself, one by one, in order not to embarrass them too much. It happened that I had in my trunk a little manual of information about such matters, intended for women, and I gave it to Mary to read. I also gave her some suffrage tracts, for I knew that her mind was ploughed up and ready for the planting. And then the next day I began very gently and delicately in a conversation with the oldest daughter to hint at the fact that great unhappiness was often caused to women by their ignorance concerning the fundamental facts of their sex nature. This eldest sister — her name was Helen — was a tall and very prim person, definitely settled into old maidenhood and church relief work. I got no response whatever to my attempts at conversation. She made it perfectly clear to me that young English women did not consider such matters suitable for conversation. I made the same attempt with the second daughter, with pretty much the same result, but I had grown a little more determined after thinking over the matter, and I went further, demanding specifically what she knew and forcing her to say that she did not know and did not wish to know. Incidentally I let slip an indiscrete hint to the effect that I had already instructed Mary, the result or which was that half an hour afterwards the mother of the house came to my room in a terrible state of agitation and proceeded to make clear to me that her daughters could not possibly take part in discussions of such ideas. "That might be the custom in America," she said, "It is certainly not in England," and she and her daughters were deeply shocked.

I asked her what her husband thought about it, and she was horrified at this. She could not mention such a subject to her husband, and when I insisted upon pointing out to her how this attitude on their part was definitely responsible for the terrible calamity which had befallen Hannah, she fell into such a state or horror and indignation that I only escaped being asked to leave the house at once by my promptness in offering to do so.

Moreover, I was watched until I had gone, and it was made clear to me that I was not to be permitted to see Mary again. My first action after leaving was to write her a letter to assure her of my friendship and support, and to tell her that if she wanted to go on and educate herself in modern ideas, I would be very glad to guide her. To this letter there came no answer. I felt sure that our friendship was not to be cut off so abruptly with Mary's consent, and after a week or so I wrote again. And about a week after that I received a letter from Mary, sent in care of my aunt. The substance of it was that she had been hoping to hear from me so as to get my address. She was very anxious to communicate with me. The books and pamphlets I had given her had been found in her room, and there had been a terrible uproar in the family, and she had been required to give her promise to have nothing more to do with me — which she had refused to do.

I saw at once what this letter meant, and as I happened to be in the city a few days later, I went to the Church where this clergyman preached, and where I knew the family invariably attended. After the service I waited in the aisle and when Mary saw me she rushed to me. I caught her by the hand and said, "I want you to know one thing. I wrote you two letters and our mail has been intercepted." That was all I had a chance to say, for then came the mother, with fire in her eyes.

"Oh, how dare you!" she whispered in a low voice, for we were in a crowded aisle, and her friends were all about her, and the world, whose opinion was law to her, was watching the scene.

"Mrs. Horton," I said, "Your daughter is of age, and she surely has a right to choose her friends."

"Please go," she exclaimed, "this is outrageous of you."

"Mary," I said over the mother's shoulder, "my address is such and so. Get word to me when you can." And then I turned and walked away, I waited after that for about a week and there came no word, and then at last one night very late there came Mary, breathless, terrified, like a hunted criminal, and she told me her story. They had taken her home, and her father in a solemn scene had demanded a pledge that she would never see me or communicate with me again. She had refused this, and so she had been confined to her room and some member of the family had been on guard day and night every since. She was to be kept a prisoner indefinitely, and the result of it was that she had taken the first opportunity to make her escape, and to come to me. She was in terror of pursuit, and was hardly to be persuaded that her family would be unable to take her back by force, that they would not call in the police for the purpose. I made sure that she was over age, and that she was willing to take what I knew would be the consequences of her refusal to obey. And then I declared that I would stand by her.

And sure enough, her father came the next morning; he had but one demand, that she should return to her home at once. Mary's answer was that she intended to do no wrong but that she was determined to have the opportunity to grow and think for herself. She was determined to continue her friendship with me and to read the books that I gave her to read, and rather then give this up she would give up her home forever. The result was that her father rose up in all his clerical majesty and in my presence solemnly banned her from the family and from his life forever. Then he took his departure, leaving the girl weeping hysterically in my arms. And that was the story of Mary Horton.

You have read her name in the newspapers, I have no doubt. I stayed in London for a month more, and during that time she read the literature of the woman's movement. She had an eager and vigorous mind, and once the old shell was broken, she grew with incredible rapidity. I found her friends in the movement in London, and before I left I saw that she had employment with money enough to keep her in a simple and decent way. She was one of those who went with the first deputation to the English Prime Minister, and she saw with her own eyes an elderly member of an ancient and honorable English family thrown down the steps of Westminster upon her head. A few days later Mary herself went to the city in which her father was preaching the faith as it had been handed down to him, and rose up in a political meeting of the Liberal party to ask the candidate his intentions on the subject of Votes for women. She was seized by the stewards and thrown out with the violence which they put into such procedure. A few days later at another meeting she chained herself to a railing and the procedure was interrupted for about twenty minutes until she was filed loose. She has been in prison about a dozen times, and has been on hunger strike two or three times, and the last letter I had from her she had been told by a physician that she was likely to die within a year or two, because of tubercular conditions which had set in as a result of injuries to the nose and throat caused by the forcible feeding procedure.

CHAPTER THREE

The Emancipated Husband:
A One-Reel Comedy

Editor's note: Like "One Woman's Fight," this one-act play takes place in Britain. In this vignette, the tables are turned as the husband proclaims his emancipation and independence to his suffragette wife. An underlying theme is Sinclair's anti-smoking and drinking attitudes, in addition to his favorite illness, dyspepsia. Two drafts of this script were found. They include a two-page abstract, and 22 pages of dialogue and stage directions. This comedy was likely written around 1912-1913 when Sinclair was in England and observed the various personalities involved in the British Woman Suffrage Movement.

[THE ABSTRACT]

The characters are Dolly Travers, an emancipated young lady, John, her husband, and Lady Evelyn, a countess. The scene is in London, and Dolly and the countess are having tea. Both are smoking cigarettes in English fashion. John comes in and manifests his displeasure at the smoking. He refuses to kiss her because of the odor of her breath. After the countess is gone they have a quarrel on the subject. John gets out an elaborate medical book and reads a terrible account of the effects of nicotine. Screen shows an illustration of degenerate nerve cells of a cigarette smoker. Another scene shows an undertaker nailing up a coffin, etc. After each one of these flashes, Dolly's anger becomes greater and greater. She tries to light another cigarette and he knocks it from her hand. She is indignant and declares that she will smoke if she pleases. They fly apart in a rage.

"The Emancipated Husband: A One-Reel Comedy," Sinclair manuscripts, Series III, Writings, Articles, Lilly Library, Indiana University, Bloomington, IN, One copy of this manuscript has "Sada Cowan, 167 Madison Ave." stamped on its cover.

Dolly is seen with the countess another day; she is smoking, and announces her emancipation. John has apparently given in and has not mentioned the subject for a week. Lady Evelyn goes upstairs and John enters. He carries a package under his arm, and pretends to be very tired. His stomach troubles him. He had been to see a doctor and the doctor has prescribed a toddy before every meal. He unwraps the package which proves to be a bottle of whiskey. His wife is dismayed because he has always been a strict teetotaler.

Screen shows him as a little boy giving a solemn promise to his mother that he would never drink. He gets some hot water, and lemon, a cork-screw, etc., and proceeds to mix himself a very large toddy. His wife is horrified. He sips it with manifestations of the keenest delight. He tries to persuade her to taste it, but she refuses with disgust. He likes it so well that he proceeds to mix himself another and drinks it off at a gulp. The wife protests in agony of soul. He proceeds to drink more and gradually manifests the symptoms of drunkenness, first becoming hilarious, waving the bottle and singing. His wife begins to weep. She tries to get the bottle away from him. He dodges around the table and drains off nearly the whole of it. Lady Evelyn appears from the other room. He continues hilarious, hales her, and invites her to drink, finally chucks her under the chin which causes her to retire and slam the door in a rage. Dolly is weeping and then John sits down at the table and begins to weep also. He admits that he is drunk. He has an inherited tendency which he cannot resist. He has been driven to it by his worry over his wife's bad habits. Dolly offers to stop smoking if he will never drink again and they shake hands over the bargain. Then John becomes suddenly sober, laughs hilariously, pour out the remaining contents of the bottle and offers it to Dolly, saying that it is nothing but sarsaparilla. Tableau of Dolly's consternation.

[THE DIALOGUE]

Characters:

> John Travers: Her Husband
> Dolly Travers: A Suffragette
> Lady Evelyn: Her "Chief"

Scene: Dolly's drawing room. At rise, Dolly and Lady E. at tea.

D: It's a terrible problem, Lady Evelyn — this having husbands.

L.E: My dear Dolly, one or the other's got to rule. Believe me, you'll never regret having taken a stand.

D: I know — but then, poor John, he's such a dear.

L.E: I know, Dolly — that's always the way. We love them so much, we just throw ourselves at their feet. And so, of course, they walk over us.

D: Yes, Lady Evelyn. But then, John is really a most exceptional man.

L.E: They invariably are, Dolly — while we're in love with them.

D: (*after a moment's thought*) Sometimes I can't help feeling as if it wasn't fair. I've attacked John in one of his more sensitive spots.

L.E: His nose, my dear?

D: (*laughs*) No, it's not merely that he objects to the smell of tobacco smoke. He objects to seeing me with what he calls a vice. He is really an extraordinarily moral man, you know.

L.E: Poor Dolly!

D: But he is, Lady Evelyn. He has the real puritanical streak in him. You see, his father drank himself to death, and his mother's always been afraid of an hereditary tendency. And so she used to pray over him, and pray to him — that he would never touch a drop of liquor while he lived.

L.E: Quite right, my dear — but drinking one's self to death is surely a different matter from smoking a cigarette now and then. It was most ridiculous for him to try and lay down such a law for you.

D: Yes, of course. (*pensively*) But he was terribly unhappy about it.

L.E: Does he still keep at you?

D: No, no — he's not that sort. When he saw my mind was made up, he stopped talking. He hasn't said a word about it for a week now. But I can feel his unhappiness.

L.E: (*grimly*) Yes — they have a way of making us feel their unhappiness.

D: No, Lady Evelyn, you're really mistaken. John's not the man to sulk. Honestly, he's behaved beautifully about the thing. I'm sometimes ashamed to have succeeded.

L.E: Yes my dear, that's always the way. I can see the outcome quite plainly.

D: What?

L.E: That he'll have his way in a week or two.

D: (*springing up*) No, he won't! No, he won't. I'm not that kind of woman at all. I've told him so, again and again! I told him before we were married. I said, "I'm an emancipated woman, a free woman." And now what does he expect?

L.E: He expects what every man expects — to be the master in his own house.

D: (*excitedly*) I said, "The house shall not be yours. I have my own money, and I'll pay for my share of everything. I don't care how much you make from your books. I intend to pay my half. I shall go right on taking part in suffrage work; I shall have my own friends and my own life." I said that, and he agreed to it; and now he sees me light a cigarette, and he has a fit.

L.E: Preposterous, my dear! Give me one.

D: (*hands her box*) I said, "Why didn't you tell me of these antiquated prejudices?" He answered "Because you never told me you smoked." I said, "I didn't smoke in those days. But now I choose to begin. Am I to understand that if you'd seen me smoking, you'd not have married me?"

L.E: What did he say to that?

D: Oh, he wouldn't answer that — he just looked wounded.

L.E: Their way, when you've had the better of them in an argument. (*offers Dolly the box*) Have one?

D: No thank you, I'll wait till John comes. You know the truth is, Lady Evelyn, I don't really care for cigarettes at all.

L.E: Is that so?

D: No, they rather make me feel sick. But it's the principle of the thing — I don't want to let myself be coerced. As I said to John, "If I once start to following the ideas you give me, what becomes of the development of my soul?" I said, "I'd far better have a vice, then be sheltered from life by a man."

L.E: Exactly, my dear!

D: He said he couldn't see why having a vice was necessary to the development of my soul; and I ought to understand how it would worry him to see me developing a vice and calling it a soul. I said, "I can only assure you that I've no remotest intention of overdoing the thing. But I mean to smoke a cigarette now and then if I see fit."

L.E: Most reasonable, surely.

D: But you see, John's a fanatic on the subject of what he considers self-indulgence. He got out a huge medical book, and read me chapters on the effects of nicotine, and the sensitive nervous organism of women. I said, "I've not the least idea of hurting myself." "But," he argued, "who ever did — at the beginning! That's always the way with these habits."

L.E: What confidence he seems to have in you!

D: That's just what I said. "John, it's perfectly insulting for you to read such stuff to me. The truth of the matter is you feel you're a weak man yourself. That's why you've such a terror about me."

L.E: (*laughing*) What did he have to say to that?

D: (*pensively*) Poor dear John! "You know how my father died," he said, "and if I have learned a little fear from it, I don't think I need to be ashamed.

L.E: He's a clever boy, isn't he?

D: The truth is, he's romantic. He thinks I'm a whole lot better than I am — and then I have to set to work to be what he thinks me.

L.E: That's one of the oldest devices, my dear; we dare not refuse to be what they love us for being.

D: He thinks of woman as an angel, and of course one can't imagine an angel who smells of tobacco.

L.E: Refuse to be an angel.

D: But he comes to kiss me — and goes away feeling sick.

L.E: It's curious — that was exactly the device his lordship, my late lamented husband, used to employ. Whenever I opposed his wishes, he'd get sick.

D: But John really has dyspepsia, you know!

L.E: In my husband's case it was asthma.

D: Oh, but Lady Evelyn, I don't want you to have a wrong idea. John has been consulting stomach specialists for years.

L.E: In my husband's case, my dear, he went so far as to die.

D: But John got his trouble by overworking so.

L.E: (*rising*) Poor Dolly! You're horribly in love, aren't you?

D: (*springing up*) I won't give in! I just won't give in! I won't be one of these sentimental, infatuated creatures! I won't be an angel! He can put me up on a pedestal as often as he pleases, but I'll jump down. I shall be what I please to be! I shall have my own friends, and I shall see them as much as I please, and let them advise me as they please —

L.E: Oh, so it's come to that!

D: What?

L.E: He thinks I'm a bad influence for you!

D: Well, naturally, you know — you understand —

L.E: (*laughing*) Go on, my dear, I don't mind.

D: Well, of course, he sees that I've grown more independent since I joined your society. And of course he disapproves of some of your ideas — John's really more old-fashioned than you could dream.

L.E: I'm sorry, my dear — perhaps I oughtn't to stay with you this evening. If your husband —

D: No, don't think of such a thing, Lady Evelyn! The idea of your wanting to desert me like that! You know how I've begged you to visit me — and this is exactly as much my house as John's. I said to him, "Lady Evelyn is a woman who could help you in all sorts of ways — if you'd be less of a monk, and more of a man of the world. She'd help you find publishers for your books, she'd introduce you to influential people. But no, "Lady Evelyn has taught me to smoke cigarettes!" I got real angry at the end, and had to shut him off. I said, "This is utter nonsense, and I won't hear a word more. I've chosen my habits and my friends — now you choose yours, and I'll have no fault to find with them. Since then, he's let me alone.

L.E: Well, my dear, I'll stay and face it out — for your sake. Its time I went up now. I want a bit of a rest before dinner. I was up till I don't know what hour this morning. This public life is hard on a woman's nerves.

D: I'll wait for John — he said he'd be in early. Adieu, my dear. (*Lady Evelyn Exit; Dolly sits at table, picks up a book, glances at it, then gets up and moves about restlessly. She hears a front door close; she listens, then lights a cigarette, goes to table, takes book and begins to read.*) (*John enters carrying package*)

J: (*cheerily*) Well, my dear?

D: Oh, so you've come.

J: (*goes to kiss Dolly, then noticing tobacco smoke, turns away to hide a face of disgust.*) (*with forced repression*) You've had tea?

D: Yes, Lady Evelyn has gone up to rest.

J: Oh! Lady Evelyn's here!

D: Will you have tea?

J: No thanks. I've had mine. I went to see Carpenter about my book.

D: Had he read it?

J: Yes, and he thinks it's great. He says I've hit it this time, Dolly.

D: (*springing up*) Oh, John, I'm so glad! John, I'll be so proud of you if you make a success!

J: Yes, it'll be rather nice, wont it! (*sits*) Dear me, I'm tired out to-day.

D: (*anxiously*) You look pale, dearest. Are you sure you're not over working?

J: No, I'm not sure. We all over work — when we are cursed with ambition.

D: But John, you <u>do</u> look pale. How was your stomach to-day?

J: Pretty good — no worse than usual.

D: What did you eat at lunch time?

J: Now, my dear — isn't that rather overdoing domesticity?

D: I know, John — but then your dyspepsia —

J: Oh, by the way I got a letter from Dr. Middleton (*pulls out letter*) He says he doesn't know what to make of my case at all — he frankly has to admit that my stomach's too much for him.

D: John!

J: Rather decent of him, don't you think?

D: But John, what are you going to do?

J: I'm blest if I know. He says I ought to stop work altogether for a while — and that I need some stimulant.

D: Some stimulant?

J: Yes — here's what he says, "I know your prejudices against alcohol, and so I don't urge you. But I honestly believe that the thing that would benefit you most of all would be a good stiff toddy before each meal."

D: Why John — how perfectly preposterous!

J: I don't know, Dolly; how can one be sure? He's the second physician who's given me that opinion.

D: But John, you can't follow it.

J: I don't know my dear. Why not?

D: But think!—

J: The fact is, I've decided to give it a trial.

D: What?

J: Yes, I'm going to see what it does for me. (*Opens package, and takes out quart bottle*) I've got some whiskey here, and I'm going to give it a chance.

D: (*horrified at the sight of the bottle*) But John, you surely don't mean that you'd drink whiskey!

J: Why, my dear — why not?

D: But John — such horrible stuff!

J: May be it's horrible and may be it's not — I've never tasted it, so how do I know?

D: But John — you've always said —

J: Have you ever tasted it, Dolly?

D: Of <u>course</u> not!

J: Then how do you know but what you'd like it?

D: But your principles!

J: That's all right, my dear. Can't one's principles change? Live and learn, is the saying.

D: But think of your promise to your mother!

J: That's all right too. But when I made that promise I was a child, and now I'm a man; I live in a man's world and I must learn to do as men do. And besides, when I made the promise, I'd never had dyspepsia.

D: John, don't make fun of me.

J: I assure you, my dear Dolly, I was never more serious in my life. I got Dr. Middleton's letter this morning, and I've been thinking it over all day. I've made up my mind that my temperance principles are old-fashioned and foolish. I'm going to learn to use alcohol in moderation, like all the other men I know.

D: But the risk, John!

J: My dear, I've not the least intention of committing excesses. I shall simply have a good stiff toddy before each meal to brace my stomach — and maybe another afterwards, if it helps. Surely there's nothing in that to worry you.

D: But remember your father! You know there's that tendency in your family!

J: My dear Dolly, do you really expect a grown man to believe ghost stories like that?

D: But John, the doctors all agree that such things happen!

J: (*haughtily*) I don't think I care to listen to any more, Dolly. If I'm not man enough to control my appetites, the sooner I find it out the better. (*Looks at watch*) An hour to dinner. That's about the right time. I think. (*Looks about the room*) May I have some of that hot water?

D: (*in agony*) John, I implore you!

J: Now my dear, please don't be absurd. (*takes large tumbler*) I wonder if this is the right sized glass?

D: John! Please listen to me!

J: I'm listening to my doctor's orders. I wonder where there's a corkscrew?

D: I can't stand seeing you do this. I shall go all to pieces.

J: A corkscrew! Oh, yes, in the table drawer. (*takes it out*)

D: Do you want to kill me outright?

J: (*stops in midst of operation*) Is this offered as a sample of the proper behavior of a modern married suffragette?

D: (*tears in her eyes*) But John, this is no ordinary matter. You've told me a thousand times how wicked you thought it —

J: Well, now I've changed my mind. Haven't I a right to change my mind? Isn't it part of the law of freedom? How can I grow, if I'm never permitted to change? (*draws cork*) Now come, Dolly, be a good girl — and if it agrees with me, you can try it too and perhaps we can learn to drink together, as other husbands and wives do. I wonder how much of this to pour? Do you think an inch is too much?

D: (*stiffly*) I'm sure I've not the least idea about it.

J: Well, I'll start with that. And then I want some sugar. Two lumps. I suppose that's enough. And then hot water. I wonder if that's all. What do you think, Dolly?

D: I tell you I've no idea!

J: You might show a little interest, at least. Dr. Middleton didn't give me directions.

D: I — I think Papa used to put a little lemon in it.

J: Oh, lemon! A good idea! I'll try that. (*takes lemon from tea-tray, squeezes it*) And now the hot water — so. That looks pretty good. (*smells*) Ah! It's not bad, I believe. (*lifts it*) Quite an adventure! Imagine a grown man — 30 years old — and never tasted a glass of grog! Well, here goes! What will it be like? (*lifts glass*)

D: John! John!

J: (*puts down glass*) What is it?

D: John, I implore you! Don't, <u>don't</u>! Stop, before it's too late!

J: (*solemnly*) Dolly, do you realize that you are interfering with the development of my soul?

D: Your <u>soul</u>?

J: Yes, my soul. I'm trying for the first time in my life to be a free, responsible individual, and you're trying to thwart me! What is the use of all your professions, if you break down at a test like this? What do you mean by talking about freedom, anyway? Are all the women to be free, and all the men slaves? What am I doing to interfere with <u>your</u> rights?

D: But John, I <u>love</u> you!

J: Don't I pay for half the house? And then haven't I the right to drink a toddy in it? The next thing you'll be trying to take away my vote! (*Dolly sinks back crushed and he lifts glass and smells*) Ah! (*tastes it, very cautiously*) Um. Why, that's not so bad! (*tastes again*) Why, I could learn to like that. Good stuff! Yes indeed! What I've been missing all these years! (*swallows some*) The very thing for me, I feel. Warms you up. Stomach better already. Ah, say, that's the real thing. No more lemonade for me! By Jove. I feel like a new man. (*taking the drink a little at a time*) Say, you've no idea how really good that is.

D: Thanks, I don't want any idea.

J: Now don't be silly, dear. (*offers glass*) If you'll only try —

D: Please be so good as to let me alone, John! (*takes book*)

J: Oh, very well, if that's the way you feel. But it seems to me when a man has suffered with his stomach as many years as I have — Oh well, never mind — I've a way of consoling myself now! (*finishing*) Ah, ah — that's the solution of my problem beyond a doubt. (*puts down glass, stands with hands on his stomach*) Yes, the very thing! Works like magic! Makes a glow all through you! Why, I feel changed all in one minute. Jolly! Full of life! Want to laugh — make jokes — have a good time! Wish I had some company though! Smoke up, won't you, old girl — that'll be a little sociable, anyhow.

D: I asked you kindly to let me alone, sir. (*reads*)

J: Oh, very well — excuse me. I'll have my toddies at the club after this. I wonder how a cigarette would strike me?

D: John!

J: Hey? (*she reads again*) I'll see (*takes one and lights it*) I don't know — poor brand, I think. I'll try a pipe some day. (*takes up bottle*) Little Rosebud Brand! Humph — rather flowery. A rose by any other name would smell as sweet, however. Ha, ha, ha! I'm getting witty. (*smells*) I'll have to experiment with different brands. (*looks at watch*) Dear me — a long time to dinner. I seem to have a ravenous appetite. Who would have believed it? (*moves about*) How am I going to pass the time? Feel rather restless. Couldn't we have a song, Dolly?

65

D: I don't feel like singing, thank you.

J: Too bad! Just when I'm sociable! Wine, woman and song, you know. Dear me, I feel so good I could almost sing myself. Suppose I were to try it? (*sings*)

"For its always fair weather
When good fellows get together!"

Ha, ha, ha! What a drab and dreary life I've led always, anyhow — so deadly respectable and unexciting! This English life of ours, colorless, utterly lacking in adventure. Here I come home, day after day, like some tame domestic animal — I never realized before what a molly-coddle I've been! And all the time I've in me the yearning for adventure, the spirit of our old roving ancestors — hard fighting men, hard drinking men! Ah me! (*takes up bottle*) Little Rosebud! You're beginning to bloom, little Rosebud! I think I'll have some more.

D: (*leaping up wildly*) John, you shall not!

J: (*amazed*) I <u>shall</u> not?

D: I forbid you. I forbid you!

J: You dare to say that to me! (*proceeds to prepare another glass, talking as he does it*) We'll see whether you'll forbid or not. We'll see who's the master of my life. We'll see whether I'm to develop my soul or not!

D: (*hysterically*) John, John! You'll drive me out of my senses! (*bursts into tears*) Oh, oh, oh!

J: Gently, gently, my dear — Lady Evelyn will hear you.

D: I don't care <u>who</u> hears me! Oh, oh, oh!

J: (*finishes pouring and tastes*) Ah, a little stronger this time. Better so, I think. Quicker action. What a joy I've been missing all these years — the realest joy in life! (*drinks about half*)

D: (*looks up with streaming eyes; in an intense voice*) John, do you realize what you're doing?

J: What, my dear?

D: You're getting drunk!

J: What?

D: You're getting drunk!

J: Why, what an idea! Me drunk? Ho, ho, ho! Ho, ho, ho! John Travers drunk! Oh Lord — imagine it! Ho, ho, ho, ho, ho, ho!

D: John, you <u>are</u> drunk already!

J: What? Drink already? Ha, ha, ha! Why, Dolly, that's the funniest joke I ever heard! (*sinks back in chair*) Ye Gods, ye gods! John Travers drunk! (*finishes glass*) Ah!

D: John, do you think you <u>couldn't</u> get drunk? Is that your idea?

J: Couldn't? Why I'm sure, my dear, I don't know. I never thought of it. I suppose I could, if I drank enough.

D: Enough! Look at the quantity you've had!

J: Not so much, my dear, really. The doctor said a glass of toddy.

D: But that doesn't mean a glass of <u>whiskey</u>, John!

J: Why not? How do you know? I think he meant a glass of whiskey, and the water and other things extra. I don't think I've had enough yet. (*takes bottle*)

D: John, stop!

J: Dolly, I thought you called yourself a suffragette!

D: John, I'll scream!

J: Ah, that's better — that's really like a suffragette.

D: John, you are a brute!

J: Of course, my dear. I am a man. (*he pours out a full glass*) I wonder how it tastes raw. (*starts to taste*)

D: Oh, you shan't! (*rushes at him*)

J: Shan't I? What's the reason? (*holding bottle and glass away from her*) Easy there, my dear. The brute might be dangerous.

D: John, if you have one particle of love for me —

J: I've a lot of love for you, my dear, but I've still more love for my right of self development.

D: John, give me that bottle!

J: Give it to you? Why, I've been begging you to have some all along. (*She seizes the bottle with both hands; he lets her have it and dodges behind the table with the full glass*) This'll do me till after dinner, I guess.

D: John, I implore you —

J: Why, aren't you satisfied? There's more than a pint there for you! Let's me see how it is. (*tastes*) Um — that is raw! (*makes face*) But I think I could get used to it. I must be a man worth of my forefathers.

D: Please, please!

J: (*he dodges, keeping centre table between them*) Here goes! Down with it. (*he gulps it, running behind table to avoid Dolly, until he has finished the glass*) There! That ought to fix any man's stomach! Now, I think I've won my spurs. (*gives her the empty glass*)

D: John, how <u>could</u> you!

J: Very easily, my dear. I've a long line of ancestors behind me.

D: It will kill you!

J: Well, at least I'll die with my boots on! (*Sings*) Sixteen men on a dead man's chest! Yo, ho, ho, and a bottle of rum! Yo, ho, ho, that's the song for a pirate! That was the real stuff that time! And now I'm feeling my oats! I want to fight somebody! I want to try my mettle! (*smites himself on the chest*) Whoop! Who-oo-oop!

D: John, you forget that Lady Evelyn is in the house!

J: Lady Evelyn! Ho, ho! I'd forgotten her. Where is she? Bring her out and give her a drop of Rosebud. She's a game old chicken.

D: John, you <u>are</u> drunk!

J: Drunk! Drunk? By the Lord Harry, I shouldn't wonder if I am! Well, whatever I am, it's jolly good fun, and I wish you felt like it. Ho, ho, Lady Evelyn! (*starts to door*)

D: John, you shall not!

J: Get out of my way! (*opens door and calls*) Yo, ho, Lady Evelyn! Where are you? Hello, Evy, old girl. Come down and have a drop of little Rosebud.

D: (*wrings her hands*) Oh, horrible!

J: I say, come down and have a toddy. Come and get Dolly to have one — the little Puritan won't drink with her husband. Come on, old girl. I'm feeling lonesome. We'll make a night of it — the three of us together. Whiskey and hot water, lemon and sugar — that's the racket. Oh, we won't go home till morning, we won't go home till morning.

We won't go him till morning, till daylight doth appear! Who-oo-oop! (*returning to room*) I guess that'll fetch her. Cordial enough, any how — hey, what do you think, little girl? (*chucks Dolly under chin*) Are you my little wifey? Hey, my dovey? Give me a kiss, little Rosebud!

D: (*shrinking in horror*) You breath is foul!

J: Oh, you don't like the smell of whiskey? Well, well — you ought to have had a drink yourself — then you wouldn't notice it! Or smoke a few more cigarettes, and it would be all right.

D: (*sobbing*) Oh, John, have you turned into a demon?

J: (*maudlin*) What — I a demon? Why, you blessed little Rosebud, I'm your own John — your lovey-dovey, tootsie wootsie sweetheart! Bless her little angel heart, she <u>was</u> unhappy! (*seizes her and kisses her in spite of her struggles*)

D: Oh, you beast! (*striking at him*) Get away!

L.E: (*in doorway*) In heaven name, what does this mean?

J: Oh, Evy! Hello Evy!

L.E: <u>Sir</u>?

D: Oh, Lady Evelyn, he's drunk!

L.E: <u>Drunk</u>?

D: Yes, drunk! He's swallowed nearly a pint of whiskey! God, what shall I do?

L.E: John Travers, is this true?

J: Why of course its true. Why shouldn't it be true? Have one, old girl? Get it from Dolly, she's got the bottle — took it away from me. And now she's angry, and she struck me. She's a cruel hard woman and she doesn't really love me. I've know it all along — ever since I've married her. She's been merciless to me. (*sobs*) She has no idea what a delicate nature I have! (*sinks by table and begins to weep*) What a poor, lonely unhappy man I am — what a sorrowful nature — how hard I have to struggle to keep myself going — to keep from committing suicide! I'm so lonely and wretched, I am — and my stomach won't digest anything — and when I take a doctor's advice and try a toddy, I get drunk — and then my wife won't kiss me — and she calls me a brute and a beast, and what can I do? I've always known I'd end up in a suicide's grave — or die a drunkard, like my poor, poor, poor, unhappy lonely father. I had only one hope — the woman I loved — yes, truly loved — but she makes my home a place of torment! — she has so many principles that she won't allow herself to love me — and so I'm driven to drink and destruction — to the bottomless pit of ruin and degradation —

D: (*moves suddenly to place behind John's chair*) Lady Evelyn, I am extremely sorry that you should have had to witness a scene so humiliating at this. I hope you will excuse me if I ask you not to witness any more of it.

L.E: Oh, certainly my dear. (*EXIT*)

D: (*with great resolution*) Now John, listen to me. You are entirely mistaken about this. It's all a cruel misunderstanding.

J: Misunnerstannin'? What cher mean?

D: You have taken this dreadful stuff, and you can't understand me now, perhaps —

J: (*bridling*) Sure I can understan'. What's reason can't understan'?

D: Oh, John, don't — Don't talk that way (*Aside, in agony*) This is the man I love, my beautiful, pure angel! (*to him*) John dear, I love you!

J: Love me! Queer kinder lover — won't lemme kiss!

D: But John, your breath is horrible now!

J: Well, so's your breath horrible.

D: Surely tobacco isn't as bad as whiskey!

J: Worse! Lot's worse! I <u>like</u> whiskey! I <u>hate</u> tobacco!

D: John, don't let's argue! I don't want to argue —

J: Never do wanne argue — when I get the best of it!

D: Listen to me, before it's too late. I want you to realize that I love you — honestly, honestly. We must not have this dreadful thing happen again.

J: Why muss'n we? Hey? Who's a-goin' innerfere my freedom?

D: Dearest, it isn't a question of freedom —

J: Yes, it's that. I'm a man, I am, a free born Englishman, and this is my castle, and every Englishman's got a right to get drunk in his own castle.

D: But John, there's no question of rights —

J: Yes, it's jes' that — question funnamental rights. I got jes' much right to drink's you have to smoke — an' what's more, I'm goin' to do it!

D: John, listen to me. Is that what is troubling you? Is it my smoking cigarettes?

J: Maybe, maybe not. Ain't sure — only know I'm unhappy. Home's unhappy, soul's unhappy, stomach's unhappy — drown my sorrows in drink.

D: John, suppose I promise <u>not</u> to smoke?

J: Hey? What's that?

D: Suppose I promise never to smoke another cigarette?

J: Wouldn't keep promise.

D: But John, I would — I'd give you my word of honor.

J: Couldn't keep word of honor.

D: But I could, I could! I don't really like cigarettes at all.

J: What cher smoke 'em for, then?

D: I smoked them because — because I was a fool, dear!

J: Well, so'm I a fool. All fools! Dam fools together!

D: John, listen to me. Will you make this bargain with me. If I stop smoking, will you stop drinking?

J: (*looking up at her sharply*) You mean that?

D: Yes, I mean it.

J: Really?

D: Yes, really!

J: Your word of honor?

D: My word of honor.

J: But you'll try to go back on it.

D: No — never! As sure as I live and as sure as I love you, if you'll promise never to drink another drop of whiskey, I'll promise never to touch another cigarette.

J: Nor a cigar?

D: No, nor a cigar.

J: Nor a pipe?

D: No, nor a pipe.

J: No chewin' tobacco?

D: No chewing tobacco.

J: On your honor.

D: On my honor.

J: It's a bargain. (*becoming instantly sober and calm*) That's all right now. I thank you very much, my dear.

D: (*bewildered*) Why —

J: (*smiling*) You can kiss me now dearest. (*kisses her*) What a relief, to be sure!

D: But, John —

J: It's all right, Dolly — I'm perfectly sober now. Where is that bottle? (*goes and takes it*) We might as well drink up the rest.

D: But what — I don't understand you!

J: (*pours out a glassful*) Here, my love, you finish it.

D: What do you mean, John?

J: It won't hurt you, Dolly. It's nothing but ginger beer.

D: (*horrified*) John!

[THE END]

PART II

Defying Sexual Convention

"You — you proposed?" stammered Algernon.

"Of course," said Lois, with a smile. "When woman is free, she will do most of the proposing. Did you never think of that?" — Upton Sinclair, *Little Algernon Fragments*, Sinclair mss., Lilly Library, ca. 1910

CHAPTER FOUR

An Unmarried Mother

Editor's note: Two copies of this 19 page manuscript were found. On the title page was typed: "Gulfport, Mississippi; 6,000 words; Copyright, 1915, by the author: all rights reserved." Curiously, the same story with another name, "The Borrowed Baby," was found in another file box. Under this name five drafts of differing lengths were found. One of these drafts had a line drawn through a handwritten "Gulfport" in the upper right hand corner. Under it "Coronado, Col." was written by hand.

The story in both versions is seen through the eyes of a governess, Miss Julia Rivington. The protagonist of the story, Harriet Edgeworth, hatches a plan to arrange for her cousin to marry the woman with whom he fathered a child. Underlying themes include the double standard of sexuality between men and women and between social classes. The lack of sex education and keeping youth ignorant of sexuality is also mentioned. Due to these themes, this story may have been an uncomfortable tale for some readers of the era.

[I]

I was waiting for Harriet Edgeworth to arrive, because I wanted to put her into a play. I needed a heroine with some advanced ideas on the subject of capital and labor, and Harriet was coming home, so she wrote, to solve the problem by turning her cotton-mills over to her employees. That sounded both advanced and heroic; so I was only waiting to see what changes a four years' stay in England had made in my former pupil. But the day before she landed, Lucy Herrick came to see me, and the story she told me drove all imaginary dramas out of my head.

I must explain that Lucy was an adopted daughter of Harriet Edge-

---

"An Unmarried Mother," Sinclair manuscripts, Series III, Writings, Articles, Lilly Library, Indiana University, Bloomington, IN. "The Borrowed Baby" was found in another folder.

worth's uncle and aunt. She had been brought up in the Massachusetts town where the mills were located, and I remembered her as a demure and timid little school-girl, with long brown pigtails hanging down her back, regarded as a member, and yet not quite a member, of a rich and important family. They were kind to her, yet thought it proper for her to make herself useful — something about which the real members of the family did not trouble themselves. I found her now, a girl of nineteen, attractive in a quiet way, somberly dressed, very pale, and obviously in trouble. She made a pitiful effort to make conversation, and to pretend that she had merely come to pay a call upon Harriet's friend and former governess. Then suddenly I held out my hands to her, and said, "Lucy, you aren't happy. What's the matter?" The tears sprang into her eyes, and she cried, "Oh, Miss Rivington, you haven't heard?"

"No, Lucy," I said, "I haven't heard anything. What is it?"

With a little tact and patience I got the story. She had been turned out of the family, and for the last six of seven months had been living in a boarding-house in New York, absolutely friendless and alone — the reasons being the discovery of a love affair between her and Ned Edgeworth, the eldest son of the family, a boy two or three years older than she, and decidedly more posted in the ways of the world. Mr. and Mrs. Edgeworth had done what they had to, said Lucy, with pitiful humility; she had done wrong, and it was impossible for them to see her any more.

At first I did not understand; she was such a child, and so obviously innocent. I thought that her offense had been her presumption in failing to realize the difference between an adopted and a real child of a well-to-do family. I had to do some cross-questioning before I got the truth. With her eyes downcast and her voice scarcely audible, Lucy made me understand that she was a mother; and that the goodness of her foster-father and mother had included giving her the name of a private hospital in the great city, and the money to pay her expenses there, and also fifteen dollars a week for as long as she needed it.

But strange as it might seem, that had not sufficed to make her happy. Two months after the birth of the child, being in utter desperation, she had thought of me, as someone who might be willing to say a human word to her. As she sobbed out the story of the insults she had had to face in her dingy boarding house, I made haste to put my arms about her, and make clear that she had one friend left in the world.

"And soon you'll have two," I added. "Harriet will be here tomorrow."

She started, and cried "Oh, no!"

"But why not?"

"I promised them that I wouldn't see Harriet — that I would never let her know about this."

"But why did you make such a promise."

"It would make her unhappy; and it's not the sort of thing for other girls to know about."

"I could not help smiling, recognizing in the phrase the piety of Mrs. Jonathan Edgeworth, Harriet's aunt; also, I thought that I recognized a little of the great lady's hypocrisy. She must have known perfectly well that her niece was a modern young woman, familiar with matters about which her feminine ancestors made pretense of ignorance. She could hardly have imagined that a girl could take part in suffrage work in London to the extent of a couple of jail sentences, without hearing stories of feminine degradation worse than poor little Lucy's.

"My dear," I said, "Harriet is twenty-three years old, and her own mistress. She will be the person to fight your battle —"

But I could not get any farther. Lucy had no idea of having a battle fought for her. She had given a promise. And so I had to give my promise in turn. But it was one that I did not mean to keep too literally!

II

I went up that afternoon to the dingy boarding-house, where I found a lovely baby-boy, in charge of an unlovely landlady. After much argument I induced Lucy to pack up her belongings, and let me find an expressman to move them down to the spare bedroom in my little apartment, she would be safe, even if Harriet were to come to see me.

And next morning I went to meet the steamer. It was a cold winter day, and I stood about and stamped my feet, looking for Mr. and Mrs. Jonathan Edgeworth. (I ought perhaps to state that Harriet was an orphan, and these two her nearest relatives.) They were not at the pier — a circumstance which I attributed to a heavy snow-storm of the night before, which had delayed traffic between New York and Boston. I made out my friend on the deck of the vessel, looking very lovely in her warm furs; and when the preliminaries were over, and the gang-plank was down, we fled to one another's arms.

At a hotel she left her baggage and her maid, with a message for her relations when they should arrive; then I carried her off to my apartment. I was full of a scheme, which kept me chattering to hide my excitement. I got Harriet settled in my front room, and then went back and sent Lucy on some errand to the kitchen in the rear; after which I deliberately spilled a glass of cold water over the baby. The yell which followed, brought Harriet running from one direction, and Lucy from the other, so that they met face to face at the bed-room door. I withdrew, leaving them to work things out as best they could.

III

When Harriet came to me again she looked very grave, and I knew that she had learned the secret. She seated herself in a chair and began, "Julia, you didn't really mean to keep all this from me!"

"Why do you ask that," I inquired.

"Nothing, except that you were always a person I could rely on."

I smiled. "What are you going to do?"

"I want a little time to think it over," she said. And sat gazing before her, her brows knitted. Somehow the very silence seemed tumultuous.

"Julia," she began, suddenly, "they turned that child out, and told her it was because she was bad! And it really isn't that at all. It's because she's poor."

"That amounts to the same thing with some people," I suggested.

"But Aunt Mary and Uncle Jonathan are Christians. At least they think they are — and all the town thinks it! And listen, Julia. Those two people have only one ambition in life just now — that I should marry Ned. Uncle Jonathan is only a minority stock-holder, you know. The control of the mills belong to me."

"I perceive the connection," I replied.

"They sent Ned over to London twice to see me. He's not a bad fellow, you know, and he soon let out the secret of his coming."

"What's his attitude to Lucy?" I inquired.

"She says he wanted to marry her. He's really a decent fellow. The last trip abroad was to get him away until she was gone. Do you wonder I am furious?"

"Not in the least," I said. And again there was a silence. Harriet had an aspect which spoke her character in every line — alertness and determination; and just now I could see the light of battle in her eyes. Suddenly I saw her stop and stare at me — or rather at some idea which had leaped to her out of space. "Julia, I have it," she cried.

"What have you?"

"The way to teach my uncle and aunt a little Christianity!"

"Tell me," I said.

"But she answered, "No, Julia. It would shock you too much! You'd better watch and see it happen."

IV

Late that afternoon came a telephone call from Uncle Jonathan, the train from Boston having just got in. Harriet invited the couple to my home, and laid down precisely my instructions that I was to agree to everything she said. Lucy was to be shut up in the far distant kitchen, and nothing less than an alarm of fire was to cause her to unlock the door.

It had been some years since I had seen Mr. and Mrs. Jonathan Edgeworth, of Mill Centre, Mass., but they had both come to the period where age does not change people — they become impervious, not merely to ideas, but to fashions. Uncle Jonathan was tall, severe in aspect, with grey side-whiskers, and you were prepared to learn that he was a pillar of a church. Aunt Mary was voluminous, dressed in black, and aware of the importance of everything she said or did. Nor is that said in a spirit of caricature; if you had lived a while in Mill Centre you would have realized that many people were modeling their costume, conversation and conduct upon the patterns which Mrs. Jonathan Edgeworth deliberately set for them.

They decorously embraced their long absent niece, and then seated themselves. In the conversation which followed a stiff anxiety became quickly apparent; for Harriet had been exposed to strange influences, unknown and even inconceivable to Mill Centre. It that time the fashion of the sons and daughters of the best families receiving jail-sentences had not even reached New York.

They wanted to know Harriet's plans, and she said she was ready to return with them at once. She asked about home people, marriages and deaths. Then suddenly she exclaimed: "Oh! I haven't shown you my baby!"

The two old people started visibly, I suppose I started also.

"<u>Baby</u>?" said Mrs. Edgeworth, with a rising inflection.

"Why yes," said Harriet. "<u>My</u> baby."

There was a pause. "You — you've adopted a child?" inquired Uncle Jonathan.

"No, no," said Harriet — It's my own child." Then I saw in one wild moment my friend's diabolical purpose.

I saw at the same time the old couple turning slowly to stone. "My dear," said the aunt, "we were not aware — you apparently did not consider it necessary to tell me us that you were married.

"Oh, but I'm not married," was Harriet's reply.

They were sitting forward in their chairs now — like two people who have just seen a ghost come into the room. They could not achieve utterance; they could only peer forward at this ghost, and through it, and then peer at each other, to see it the other had seen it. It was a hideous and terrifying spectre; but Harriet sat smiling, as if not aware of its presence.

"My dear," stammered her aunt, at last, "I — I really don't understand."

"What is there to understand, Aunt Mary? Did you never hear of an unmarried mother?"

Again there was a pause. I would have felt sorry for these two tormented souls, if I had not had my mind made up that they were incapable of suffering more than they deserved to suffer.

At last Harriet seemed to become aware of the tension. "It's really nothing to be surprised about," she said. "It's quite the fashion nowadays — the very best people do it."

"Good God!" ejaculated Mr. Edgeworth — but not irreverently.

"You see," continued the girl, "it was in London. No one believes in marriage any more in London. Haven't you read Bernard Shaw?"

Suddenly Mrs. Edgeworth exploded, into a sort of scream, "Harriet! How dare you!"

"My dear," put in Uncle Jonathan, more mildly, "is this some joke that you are playing on us?

His niece sprang up. "Wait a minute. I'll show you."

As she went past my chair, she gave me a terrifying frown. Left alone with Mr. and Mrs. Jonathan Edgeworth, I saw their horror-smitten eyes turn towards me. I was the person to waken them from this night-mare! I was an American, and a lady, after a fashion — had I not been a duly certified governess in their family for many years? Surely I could not now be sitting there, playing a part in this nightmare!

Mr. Edgeworth had just cleared his throat to address me, and I had begun to squirm in my seat, when Harriet came back with a bundle of whiteness in her arms. "Little Jonathan!" she said — and apparently did not notice how they started and blazed with wrath. "Little Jonathan!" The blasphemy of it!

Holding the precious burden in her arms, she seated herself and smiled down upon it in orthodox, happy-mother fashion. "He's going to be so lovely," she murmured. "His father is as handsome as a god."

"Oh, indeed!" snorted Mrs. Edgeworth; and then, with freezing politeness, "May I presume to ask why you did not marry the gentleman?"

"Oh, it wouldn't have done at all, Auntie. In the first place, he's poor, and you wouldn't have considered him a desirable party."

"It isn't a question of desirability, Harriet — it's a question of morality."

"But it would have been unpleasant, Auntie! His relatives were outraged at the idea. For, you see, I was a nouveau riche American to them."

"Give me his name," cried Mrs. Edgeworth, in a passion.

"Ah, but I promised not to. It would not be just to him."

"He deserves no justice! The cowardly wretch — to ask such a promise from a woman!"

Harriet rose, baby and all.

"Aunt Mary!" she said, in a voice which stopped the torrent suddenly. "Aunt Mary, please understand me. I do not permit any one to speak in that fashion of the father of my child."

"You mean," cried the other, "that you expect me to tolerate this outrageous —"

"Aunt Mary, if you persist, you will make it necessary for me to leave the room."

Where as Mrs. Edgeworth boiled over, "You may spare yourself. If this is what you have come to, it is we who should leave the room." And she seized her hat and wraps, entirely without heeding their shape or dignity. "Come Jonathan," she said.

"But, my dear —" stammered he.

"Jonathan, <u>come</u>!" she said, in a voice which is obeyed by husbands of ladies of social position. He took his hat, made a feeble start at a sort of farewell, and then, giving it up, followed his wife our of the door.

V

I did not believe that they would ever come again; but Harriet laughed at me. "I am the majority stock-holder," she said.

And sure enough, that evening Mr. Edgeworth telephoned to ask if he might see her for a few minutes. "He said 'upon a matter of business,'" she added, with a smile.

When Mr. Edgeworth arrived, I offered to retire, but Harriet bade me remain. And after clearing his throat several times, he began:

"Harriet, your aunt and I have talked this matter over, and have decided that we will make no effort to interfere with what you consider your own affairs. The request we have to make of you concerns ourselves alone. If there are people in England who approve of-or-your ideas, that is presumably their affair. But in America such is not the case. So we wish to beg that you will manage somehow not to let the truth be known while you are in this country."

"But Uncle Jonathan, that is unthinkable. Secrecy is the last thing in the world that I could tolerate."

"Why so?"

"You don't understand, apparently, that I am engaged in an act of propaganda. I am doing something which I believe is proper, and which I wish other people to know about and imitate."

"And you will pay no attention to the feelings of those particular people — your relatives — who surely have most claim on you?"

They debated for several minutes; until suddenly the old man turned to me. "Miss Rivington," he said, "surely you must be able to understand my point of view."

"I understand it," I replied, "but also I understand Harriet's; and I would not feel myself competent to mediate between them." This little speech I had been made to learn by heart, and it had the desired effect of keeping me on the spectator's bench.

"Uncle Jonathan," said Harriet, "I could not grant your request even if I wanted to, for there is the far more important problem of the mills which calls me home."

"You mean that actually you contemplate coming to Mill Centre with your — your baby?"

"Certainly, Uncle Jonathan."

"You must surely realize, Harriet, that that could have only one effect — to drive you aunt and myself away from our home forever."

"Well, Uncle Jonathan —" She paused. "I don't want to say anything that might even seem unkind. But it is really a fact that the new era which is coming to the mills will be one which you will not approve. I think you might be happier if you washed your hands of it altogether."

There was a pause. "Would you mind, Harriet, give me some idea of the changes you propose carrying out in the management of the mills?"

I saw Harriet's glance flicker for one instant at me.

"I think," she said, "that we had better wait till I am comfortably settled at home, before we attempt to consider questions of business. I will only throw out this one hint to you — that Ned has met some advanced people in London, and picked up a few ideas — I saw to that. So it may be that he will find it possible to adjust himself to what I have in mind."

But this crumb of comfort did not last Mr. Edgeworth very long. "That is one point which your aunt has asked me to mention. She is especially anxious that this situation should not be made known to Ned. You can readily understand that the effect upon a young man's mind might be — well — er — not beneficial."

"Why, really, Uncle Jonathan," said Harriet — "can you for one moment imagine that Ned is uninformed about such matters?"

"I have not made any effort to know the extent of my son's information —"

"You should have done so, Uncle Jonathan. That is one of the first and most important duties of a father, and many misfortunes result from his failure in it. How do you know but Ned may have adopted the same ideas as myself?"

She was as sober as any propagandist, and the other showed no gleam of suspicion. "I am quite sure," he said, pompously, "that my son — has not to put it offensively —"

"That he has not adopted my ideas."

"Precisely."

"But you are afraid that he might be led to adopt them?"

"No, no — but —"

"You simply don't care to have his associate with an unmarried mother."

"Well, since you put it that way —"

"You don't."

"I don't."

Harriet pondered. "Suppose, Uncle Jonathan, that it were a question of his associating with an unmarried father."

There was a pause. "Er —" said Mr. Edgeworth.

"You understand, of course, that for every unmarried mother there is also an unmarried father — at any rate, a father who is not married to that mother. And what I want to know is, if you consider such a man a proper associate for Ned."

"I should certainly not so consider him — if I knew it."

"Ah! If you knew it! But if you did not know it, then it would be all right?"

"If I did not know it," said Mr. Edgeworth, solemnly, "I should not know it."

"And now," said Harriet, with a gentle smile, "you have expounded to me the basis of all bourgeois morality. There is one sin in the world, which is to have it known."

After a pause she suddenly rose. "Uncle Jonathan, I cannot see that there is anything to be gained by our going on with this discussion. I can give you my definite answer. I am coming to Mill Centre tomorrow or the day after, because I have some important work to do there. I shall bring my baby, because a baby belongs with its mother; also because of my conception of morality, which is that the worst of all offenses is to conceal and pretend. Finally I must tell you I shall make no effort to preserve Ned's innocence. He is old enough to know the facts of life. Moreover, I want to talk over with him the possibility of his taking charge of the mills and helping to carry out the plans which I have in mind."

VI

"They will ship Ned away," I predicted; but Harriet laughed at me again. "Didn't you hear me offer him a job?"

"Then what will they do?"

"I don't know, But they will do something, and quickly — before I start for home."

And sure enough, the next morning at nine o'clock came a telephone call from a gentlemen who announced himself as the Reverend Harrison Fordsworth, Protestant-Episcopal rector at Mill Centre. He inquired if he might be allowed to call, and Harriet assented. To me she remarked, "They must have used the telephone and brought him down on the midnight train!"

"Do you know him?" I asked.

"No — he's a newcomer. The old rector died last year."

I had an engagement that morning, and when I came back to lunch Harriet told me the story of the interview. She had been prepared for some old fogy, and instead had come what she described as "an infant," pink checked and innocent, blushing furiously, and most dreadfully embarrassed by the errand upon which he had been sent.

She said: "I had the campaign all prepared; as soon as he began to speak to me with authority, I told him that I had no respect for his profession — that I regarded him as a parasite, taking the money of the rich to preach submission to the poor. And what do you think he said to that? It seems, my dear, that he's a Christian Socialist, one of our modern St. Crysostoms! Imagine the cunning of my uncle!"

"But what's he been doing in Mill Centre?"

"He's been causing almost as much trouble there as I could wish. Uncle Jonathan had just arranged everything to have him fired, when this new matter turned up. So he sent for him this morning, and told him that if he would settle this, he might preach fire and dynamite in Mill Centre forever after."

"And how did he make out?"

"He was rather clever," she smiled. "He began at me with Kant's rule of Practical Reason. 'Act so that you will be willing for your course to be adopted as a general rule by all mankind.' 'You, Miss Edgeworth,' he said, 'are in a position to afford the indulgence in certain luxuries, which are beyond the girls who work in your mills. You might be the means of leading some of them to ruin.' You can see that was a hard argument for me to answer."

"What did you do?"

"I told him the truth."

85

"The <u>truth</u>!"

My friend had begun to turn color, and here she burst into laughter. "The situation was impossible, Julia. I could play this game with my uncle and aunt, because I feel contempt for them. But how could I play it with a young disciple of muscular Christianity, who I might be tempted to fall in love with?

"But are you sure you could trust him with the secret?" I asked.

"The end I have in mind," she said, "is perfectly orthodox, in line with his Christian duty. I sent him back to tell the family he could do nothing with me — I persist in my intention of going to Mill Centre this afternoon."

"And what will happen next?"

"I am expecting to hear from Aunt Mary," said Harriet. And sure enough, before we had finished lunch, the telephone rang.

VII

It was a much subdued and chastened Mrs. Jonathan Edgeworth who paid this second call. She proceeded with hardly any preliminaries, to throw herself upon her knees. She was old, and so was her husband; the shame and terror of this thing were breaking them. They would be driven from their homes, it would kill them both. Was there not some way, out of simple human pity, for Harriet to spare them this unthinkable humiliation?

Harriet was unable to think of a way. Could they suggest one?

They could, it appeared. The suggestion might startle her at first; but if she would stop and consider, she might see its advantages. They wanted her to marry her cousin Ned!

Mrs. Edgeworth rushed on, as if she were afraid of being ordered from the room. "Please hear what I have to say! Ned was abroad on two occasions, and so it would be quite plausible to say that you two have been secretly married. And then — then — if you don't care for Ned, your marriage can be merely in name, and after a decent interval, say two or three years, you can obtain a divorce, and thus spare us all this agony."

"But Aunt Mary, you astonish me! I thought you disapproved of divorce!"

"I have disapproved of it — I disapprove of it yet. But — but —"

"You disapprove still more of scandal?"

"You are always so hard to argue with, Harriet!"

"But don't you see, Aunt Mary, what it would lead to? You teach that for a divorced person to re-marry is a mortal sin. So I should be sentencing myself to celibacy for life."

"You have your own ideas about such matters, my dear; and you would act on them —"

"But the law is none the less the law, Aunt Mary — no matter what my ideas may be! What it amounts to is that you would be willing to see me damned, rather than face this scandal!"

There was a pause, during which Mrs. Edgeworth gulped several times. She had withenough [*sic*] to see that she was being punished — and also to see that she must take the punishment. "Yes, Harriet," she said, "I would."

"But then consider your son, and his rights in the matter. Surely I am not a fit woman to marry an upright young man!"

"You — you need not trouble about that. That is our affair."

"But let me understand you clearly. You do not consider that a woman who has born a child out of wedlock is thereby unfitted, either morally or socially, to marry your son?"

"No, I do not."

"And your son would be willing to make such a marriage?"

"I am sure he would."

"And if by such a marriage the child could be legitimized, you and Uncle Jonathan would be satisfied?"

"Yes, Harriet."

And Harriet's answer came quickly — so quickly as to strike her aunt dumb. "Very well, then," she said, "We will settle it by such a marriage. You may send Ned to see me at once, and the matter will be arranged."

VIII

They had already ordered Ned from Boston, it transpired, and he came in that evening — covered with confusion, and in general as uncomfortable a college boy as any one could imagine.

"Harriet," he began, "I — I don't know what to say —"

"Ned," she demanded quickly, "you would be willing to marry me?"

"You know perfectly well, Harriet, I never dared even fall in love with you. But if you say this is right, I suppose it is."

"And you're not ashamed of me, Ned — after what I've done? You'd consider me a proper woman to be your wife?"

"Don't talk nonsense, Harriet. I don't know anything about what you've done — but I know you have your own ideas, and that you're much too good for me. I haven't been a plaster saint myself, you know."

"That's decent of you, Ned," she said. "Now I want to ask you something personal, and I want you to answer straight."

"Fire away, old girl."

"Why don't you marry Lucy Herrick?"

He stared at her a moment; then his eyes fell, and I saw the blood rush into his neck and forehead. "You know about that?" he said, in a disappearing voice.

"I know about it Ned. I ran into her by accident. Answer my question, please."

"It's very simple, Harriet. The Pater said he'd disinherit me, that's all. I suppose I was a cad, but I didn't see how I could support her."

"Ned," said his cousin, "Lucy's been living here in New York all alone. She's the mother of a child of yours. If it's so necessary to legitimize children, it seems to me that's the place for you to begin."

There was nothing for Ned to say to the argument; and it was to his credit that he realized this. After a long silence, he remarked, "You know how it is, Harriet — when a fellow grows up without working, his father and mother are boss. And you know how it is with my father and mother. There was no question of legitimizing children — there was only the scandal, and the money."

"Suppose," said Harriet, "that some one were to offer you a job where you could do something interesting, and at the same time earn a decent living; would you be willing to marry Lucy now?"

"Yes, Harriet," he said. Then, after a moment; "You know, of course, that I'd be disinherited."

"No," replied Harriet, "I don't think that would happen. You see, your parents have said they wanted this child legitimized. And this child isn't mine at all — it's your child and Lucy's."

IX

We struck the iron while it was hot. Harriet had warned the Reverend Harrison Wordsworth that he might be needed. While we were waiting for him we sent Ned back to the kitchen to have matters out with Lucy, and to make the acquaintance of his child. When they came in to us, they looked so young, and so obviously in a whirl of emotion, that Harriet had to throw her arms about the girl and start her to weeping, and me also. I saw even the "pink-cheeked infant" — that is, the Reverend Harrison Wordsworth — wipe his eyes suspiciously.

After the ceremony we put the young couple into a taxicab, and Harriet emptied the content of her purse into their laps, and told them to set out next morning for Atlantic City. Then she summoned another cab and started for the hotel where her uncle and aunt were staying. I suggested that she put that ordeal off on me, but she would not hear of it. When she came back I discovered why.

"What happened?" I said; and she stretched her arms and gave a happy laugh.

"Oh, Julia! You've no idea of the relief! To find myself respectable again!"

I looked at her in surprise. "You were so blithesome in carrying it off," I said, "that I'd quite forgotten that view of it."

"But oh, Julia!" she cried. "Think of the picture I've had in my mind — the scenes I've been carrying about in my imagination! Of myself in Mill Centre with my 'little Jonathan'!"

CHAPTER FIVE

Eugenic
Celibate Motherhood

Editor's note: Little is know about this manuscript. The first three pages are handwritten. They appear to be the introduction for a speech to the Workers' Educational Association, an organization for adult education in Australia. However, it is unknown if it was delivered, or printed, by the association for its members. Following the handwritten pages, twelve typewritten pages of the draft are found. Two titles, "The Right to Motherhood" and "Celibate Motherhood," were typed on the first page, but were crossed out and replaces with "Eugenic Celibate" motherhood. In the body of the essay, the term "scientific motherhood" was changed to "celibate motherhood." Sinclair cites the controversial book Married Love *by Marie Stopes, published in 1918. Other references from this year, and the ending of World War I, were given, so the essay was likely written around 1918-1919.*

Two paragraphs that were crossed out of the draft are included here as they give more insight into the history and the culture of the era. They are in italics.

Sinclair promotes eugenics in this manuscript. He also promotes artificial insemination for single women as a way of increasing the population due to the war deaths. Artificial insemination for unmarried women was very controversial during this time, and is still controversial among some people today. Eugenics, "the science of improving the human race," was accepted by the educated during the first few decades of the twentieth century.

Madame President and Fellow Members of the Workers Educational Association

It is a great privilege to be able to discuss briefly this evening the suggestion of Celibate Motherhood as a remedy for one of the most poignant griefs [*sic*] of suffering womanhood — the grief of childlessness which is the

---

"Eugenic Celibate Motherhood," Sinclair Manuscripts, Series III, Writings, Articles, Lilly Library, Indiana University, Bloomington, IN.

doom of some of the noblest of women and often is their doom just because they are noble. It illustrates the intellectual timidity of Australian leaders that not one of the recognized writers or speakers or professional guides of our public has so much as hinted that any such tragedy exists in women's lives. Yet only last week in England, this topic has leapt into free and full discussion in the press, under the impetus of Miss Sarah March's assertion that women of independent means are prepared to have children without marriage. Would any Australian newspaper publish such news unless it were cabled from England? Would its editor allow such a controversy to be reproduced here?

My hope is that when the next Birthrate Commission sits in Sydney, the women who are living in the land of foremost domestic legislation, who have for years enjoyed the privilege of voting, will insist that their voice shall be heard on all subjects to do with the welfare of women and children and that the able women speakers of the Workers Educational Association will be heard on all subjects dealing with race improvement.

Coming now to our subject. The practice of artificial fertilization in a childless marriage has been resorted to for many years, and numbers of women have thus been enabled to realize the joy of motherhood. In such cases the husband is the father of the child so begotten. Doctor Stopes in her book, "Married Love," page 149 advances a new preposition that all thinking people would do well to take into their earnest consideration is the present crisis, remembering that everything that conduces to the happiness of the individual, if brought about by means that involve no deterioration of our present "mores," and that causes no other individual to suffer, must be a blessing, not only to the individual so benefited, but to mankind.

Dr. Stopes suggests that should a husband in a marriage be incapable of being a father, the wife should be impregnated from the "life" of some other man of whose identity she should be incognizant. Such a suggestion, coming from such a source, may well be examined dispassionately. Dr. Stopes does not see any reason to insist that the natural act of union between man and woman should be the only way of producing offspring. With her woman's insight and common sense, added to her wide knowledge, she truly sees that at the commencement of a new life the moment when the male cell is able to impress upon the new being, once and for all, the full attributes both physical and mental, of the father, is the crucial moment.

Psychologically, as well as physiologically, that moment is when the male cell meets the ovum in mutual fusion.

That meeting may not occur until hours, or even days after the physical act which brings human bodies and souls together in a happy marriage, and which ends with its immediate mission fulfilled, but with its ultimate purpose unattained.

The search after a new life is continued after the fleeting rapture of union until it reaches that supreme union of human cell with human cell, when mortality and immorality commingle. Then and then only is begun a new life and a new love.

It is for that meeting of human cells that the lives of men and women should be dedicated in earnest preparation from childhood. Had the natural act any special significance in controlling or transmitting the qualities of the father, the "sins of the fathers" would not cause any anxious reflection. Experience has shown that in the most happy union dignified by mutual passion, love, and respect, the offspring can inherit appalling consequences, because no emotion, however exalted, can control the operation of the inflexible law of the transmission of any disease or weakness with the parent cell.

Men and women must free themselves from the erroneous idea that mating and parenthood are synonymous. They will then be able to assure the safety and permanence of the race, by controlling both heredity and environment, which now left to themselves, sometimes conflict with one another and work tragic consequences. Conversely, the prayer, the thought, the training of a life time, added to healthy descent, cannot be nullified by an act of scientific practice in its life-conveying mission.

The healthy male cell of a good man, uniting with the healthy ovum of a good woman, must product a healthy child, endowed long before its birth with all the characteristics, both mental and physical of the two parents.

Dr. Stopes, in offering the consolation of which I have spoken to childless women who are married, knows that science has justified its acceptance and is assured of its result. Her appeal for those of her own sex who are deprived of their greatest happiness through no fault of their own, should cause men and women to dwell on this most important theme, and to go further and ask themselves whether a proposal to confer innocent motherhood upon unmarried woman by the same scientific means, should not be accepted with that generosity and broad-mindedness which Dr. Stopes has displayed.

In addition to considering the case of the married woman who is debarred from realizing that which her Maker has planted within her — the desire for children — it would be well for the public to extend its sympathy to the large number of unmarried woman, who through no fault of their own, are not only without this great happiness of motherhood, but are also without the companionship of a life partner.

It will be impossible for millions of women in the future to have "that mysterious union of mind and body, which, while it continues our species, is the source of all our affections" and which completes the condition of a true marriage. The abnormal conditions and environment in which women of the future will be placed as a result of the war, will demand a new corrective, and the public would do well to take to heart the suggestions of Dr. Stopes for those who are mated, and extend them to those for whom mating is impossible.

In peace time, too, there have been abnormal conditions which engender a preponderance of females, and society has looked on in the past at the extinction of some of the flower of our womanhood, and if the married women is to be aided in her desire for motherhood when she has the alleviating circumstances of married life to solace her for its incompleteness, we can surely not be reconciled to the double tragedy of unmarried women bereft of both consolations, and denied both motherhood and partnership.

If after sixty years of experiences of scientific artificial fertilization for married people has been accepted and proved to be sound in practice as in theory, is it not almost criminal neglect on the part of Eugenists, medical men and women, social reformers, and legislators, not to support a movement for the extension of that advance in science for those, who for various reasons, may not marry and yet would welcome a clean, wholesome motherhood such as is suggest by "Dr. Swan" in his brochure "Facultative Motherhood."

By artificially fertilization the married woman can have her hopes realized in many cases, the individual is happy, and the world is richer, and science will have seemed to have achieved still higher aims, if the body and soul of the virgin can be kept sacred while motherhood is conferred upon any who desire and deserve it.

94

Note: The writer know of one case of artificial fertilization in another country where a married woman was impregnated with the "life" from a stranger: her only stipulation was that the "life" should come from good stock. The child thus begotten is now married and has children of her own.

The desire for motherhood in women with all its physical and spiritual benefits, is not wholly understood by medical men. There is a physiological fact pertaining to women alone which is so interwoven with its psychological aspect that no man, be he a medical man of long standing and experience, student of psychology, observer of sex and marriage, or thinker on this question, can or will ever be able to understand, except so far as he learns about it from women. Apart from this source of knowledge, that fact must always carry with it a great impenetrable secret as to which Nature asks his silence while he pauses, unable to enter this Holy of Holies, conscious only of his incapacity to do more than reverence its sacred portal.

This fact which Dr. Stopes sees so clearly, which is quite apart from passion, is that subtle maternal instinct in the awaiting mother, which not only surrounds the loved being on its journey to life, but which has been transmitted from mothers to daughters through countless ages, so that in the growing and unfolding of her destiny, every woman is reminded of that mysterious insistence of her nature which impresses on her, her call to motherhood.

This has been early shown in her baby habit of hugging her doll, in her childish care of it, in her girlish love of other people's children, and afterwards in her woman's strong and full realization of that within her from childhood, when her nerves and pulses cry out for the creative union of her soul of the pre-ordained and existent being within her, which is waiting to claim its birthright.

We see this paramount instinct strongly developed in women who are lacking in passion, who are cold and unsympathetic in marriage, yet who make beautiful mothers and devoted grandmothers. These women have not the mating instinct, and do not realize their limitation in this respect. In marriage their call to mother hood is satisfied to the full; their heart's desire is complete in their children. The tragedy of an incomplete destiny in these cases is for the husband.

Again there are women who want a mate and do not want children, and lastly there are woman who want to bear children, but who do not mate for various reasons. It is to this last-named class of women that Eugenic Celibate motherhood appeals. They understand the psychology of mating and the differing psychology of motherhood, and is them the latter demands that when the creation of their nature should not be desecrated by the presence of passion without love or love without permanence.

Mating and motherhood are only interwoven so far as mating is co-existent with the love of one for one, for it is only in that dual completion of two permanent forces of love and life, that the ideal procreation in the natural way is consummated.

To this type of women no enticing legislation to sanction the increase of the illegitimate birth-rate will ever appeal. They will refuse to effect the lasting purpose of life by a moment of fleeting emotion; they will not allow the soul of motherhood to descent to a plane where memories, better unremembered, bestow no sanctification and their ideal is lost in a physical conception unhallowed by real and abiding love.

In this coming laws of Eugenic birth control, let there be that insistence of forethought for the yet unborn.

The present situation presents an appalling problem: hundreds of thousands of the flower of our womanhood will have to die out owing to the depletion of the males as a result of the war, (for the majority of the fighting men were marriageable men).

The European races emerge form a war with the flower of their manhood dead and dying, others unfit to be fathers from illness or shock or disease, and it will take centuries to retrieve this huge disaster.

Our dead for Australia number over 59,000. What is to be the destiny of the number of unmarried women who would have been wives but for the war? A sad light upon the poignancy of this question was revealed to us in the attitude of some of the Australian girls who so strongly resent the arrival of brides from other lands, who had come to take the places which might have been theirs in the hearts and homes of some of our returned soldiers. What we see in Australia is going on in other countries because human nature is everywhere the same.

A delegation of women from England will shortly arrive in Australia with the object of ascertaining whether there is a prospect of settling some of the surplus women of England on the land out here. The war is over and the Government in England see the necessity of providing something for some of the three million surplus women. Whether the delegation meets with encour-

agement as to land settlement or not for them, it seems only natural to suppose that many will come here to try their luck. Perhaps many will come to join their relations who are the wives of our soldiers, 15,000, of whom have brought English wives to our land.

So the problem for Australia reaches the point when all suggestions must be considered in seeking its solution, and Australia, like all other countries that have taken part in the war, will have to consider the needs of those who will be denied their happy position of wifehood and their rightful vocation of motherhood.

The distress of the world's maidens thus widowed by the war is all the more embittered because during the war girls have themselves done so much for their country. Nearly four years of their young lives have been spent under circumstances of sorrow and work, of heart-breaking anxiety for the loved ones going or the loved ones there, and of perpetual sorrow for those who can never return.

And are these Spartan bearers of the nation's burden of grief and labour to be compelled to die out if a nation's gratitude can prevent it? Is this fine race of women to be allowed to suffer extinction for want of public support to evolutionary and progressive methods? It is for such women that we ask the broad-minded consideration of the community to the suggestion that the way be opened for science to heal this, as well as other wounds, of our national being. It is true that more avenues of work may be opened up for women; that new paths of industrial usefulness may claim them in thousands that fresh fields of learning may welcome them to abundant harvests, and in such new endeavors we wish them God-speed.

At the same time can we say that in opening up only these various activities, we are serving the best of our womankind with all that can be done for them?

Since deprivation of wifehood must be theirs, if we are to retain monogamy, the old and well tried vocation of motherhood should also be added for those who desire it. If such women, who in the hour of their nation's danger in the past, rose in their strength to help to save her, are willing in the future to sustain and prolong her national life, shall they not be enabled to provide the nations with its greatest possession and heritage — healthy children, engendered without sin or selfishness? Can the nation afford to lose these women, as potential mothers, when the race is staggering because of vitality in part weakened by war losses, in part vitiated by war diseases?

The only alternative proposal that has been hinted at so far, to meet the problem of the great preponderance of females, is the easy expedient of illegitimacy, favored in the past by some Governments that have first made wars and then sought to replenish population by reckless legislation. It would be well for governments and those who make them, to turn the searchlight of conscience on to their camouflage of sympathy for the women who cannot marry, and see whether they will not find hidden behind it, the panic cry of food for powder, regardless of any other consideration.

Further, will the proposal to regulate the irregularity of illegitimacy provide for the registration of the fathers, married and unmarried, of illegitimate children. If it does not, how long will marriage remain one of our sacred institutions, if it does not, how will the intermarriage of consanguineous offspring be prevented? The warning voice of Eugenists has been heard on the danger of consanguineous unions where there is any bad strain, and in these days when the percentage of venereal diseases is so appalling, how can a bad strain in the offspring of illegitimate unions be eliminated with any degree of certainty.

While insisting on the physical dangers of consanguinity, once illegitimacy achieves recognition, we must also face the grave results which are bound to accrue from the outrage of noble feelings and delicate instincts which illegitimacy involves.

Can we deliberately take the backward step of legislating for increased promiscuous intercourse, that vast distributor of venereal diseases? What race improvement will follow from such a legislation? What happiness to the individual? What legacy to the child? What stability to our "mores"?

If it were conceivable in these days when women are taking an active interest in their responsibilities as guardians of the race as yet unborn, that illegitimacy or polygamy or concubinage could be sanctioned by law, we should still see the extinction of the flower of our womanhood, for the best women would rather go through life childless than consent to have a child by a man whose interest in them is only transitory. Such women will never become the means of dragging down womanhood, wifehood, and motherhood to lower ideals than those for which humanity has hitherto been striving.

I will now touch lightly upon some of the expedients proposed elsewhere to meet the tragedy of the unmarried childless woman. Polygamy or a system of collateral wives, as is said, was encouraged by the Kaiser's Government during the war, would be preferable to illegitimacy, because the wife and offspring would have name and registration.

Pen-ultimate separation again for the older wives, would be preferable to polygamy and concubinage, for the home would be kept sacred to the love of one for one, while the children of a new union were growing up.

The suggestion for Celibate Motherhood was not first thought of as a war measure, and the system could take its place with dignity beside marriage for all time if necessary, without dislocating society in the least degree. It would be the means of inspiring a motherhood based on a true Eugenic ideal, and would be its greatest aid and interpreter at a juncture when the almost tragic haste for marriage at any cost and at any price, renders the Eugenic insistence upon clean, healthy fatherhood, practically impossible.

At present there can be little hope of directing marriage along eugenically desirable lines for two obvious reasons. First, there would be so few marriages permitted, if a clean bill of health on the husband's side were to be insisted upon. Statistics prove this beyond a doubt, and for many years to come there will be grave dangers to the offspring resulting form the hurried war marriage which are being now contracted. Second, there will be such a dearth of husbands. If side by side with eugenically desirable marriages in the future, there [would] be a Eugenic Motherhood such as Scientific Motherhood, effected by a healthy though unknown fatherhood, in place of unhealthy, irresponsible parenthood, unlicensed by our present "mores" and certain to bring disastrous consequences to future generations, there would be hope where now there is little.

Scientific Motherhood, thought of in peace time for women who for one cause or another do not marry, and yet desire motherhood, cannot only graft itself on to the parent stem of Eugenics, but can help to plant it at the very root of the "mores" of society.

One of the many popular beliefs to be scrapped in sane discussions about the future, is the supposition that more males are born during war time than in peace times. This has permitted the selfish unit of society, whose only real thinking consists in an animated policy of "drift" to utter the remark that "things of that sort will right themselves."

The American Journal of Obstetrics, Volume 75, page 1079, contains a brief review of an article by Siegel. In this article Siegel discusses the male birth-rate during the war with references to the supposed preponderance of the birth of male children which followed the war of 1870. An investigation of the official statistics showed that the relation between "boys and girls was practically the same and yet the popular idea seems to favour a different version." See "Eugenical News," Volume 3, 1918. Also, under the heading of "War and Childbirth," the following appears:

"In the Medical Record, May 1918, Richter states in speaking of the decreased birthrate in lower Austria, that 'boys are not more numerous than girls.'"

The happy-go-lucky evasion of so serious a state of affairs ought not to be the attitude of the public. The urgent need for population in Australia should ensure a careful consideration of the subject of Scientific Motherhood, even if that need were the only national need; but there is a still greater claim for its acceptance — the happiness of so many individuals and the diffusion of that happiness amongst the community.

We have discussed the objections to the destructive proposals of illegitimacy, polygamy and concubinage, and it is easy to show that the constructive measure of Celibate Motherhood is free from all these objections. The lack of registration of the fathers, the consequent risk of intermarriage of the offspring, the increase of promiscuous intercourse and the spread of venereal diseases, are dangers that cannot be urged against Scientific Motherhood. As to polygamy or 'collateral' unions, the dislocation of the marriage state are the reversion to Turkish ideals have no counterpoint in a system of Celibate Motherhood.

Scientific Motherhood admittedly lacks the element of comradeship in a happy union, nor does it pretend to satisfy the mating instinct. Further, it lacks the sheltering aid of a good father in the training of the child; yet it offers a motherhood free from the objections that are linked to the alternatives, and it secures for the child a birthright that any child might be proud of, and the environment of a mother, whose natal gift to her child will be healthy breeding, whose legacy to her child will be selflessness and self-control, and whose contribution to her country will be the most valuable treasure a country can have, whose example to her fellows of stainless maternity will be an inspiration to the recovery of parenthood, whose share in race improvement will be incalculable, whose memorial to the dead will be her vow loyally kept that as far as she is concerned, only those shall be borne who will be as worthy as those who lie in the East and in the West.

It is for women to choose this new path of happiness and usefulness only if they desire it. It is the duty of the community to see that the way is ready for them as occasion of the lengthening course of the time may reveal a desire for its acceptance.

It should be the privilege of the medical profession to further its advent as soon as possible in order that no potential mother need be disappointed in her wish to have a child, and so hasten this advance in science (which sooner or later is bound to come) that it may not be too late for the many that may welcome it and deserve it.

The methods of artificial insemination are simple, innocuous and safe, and have been recognized and gratefully accepted by married people for many years. The Institute which will be specially designed to meet all requirements in order to safeguard the mothers and their children, will be controlled by men and women not only of high scientific skill, but of known moral reputation. The request for the co-operation with the Institute of married healthy people, will be made known will all necessary delicacy and need cause no comment.

It is proposed that only married people whose children are grown up shall be asked to contribute the "life." A healthy man of 50 can produce a perfectly healthy child, and this alone would make the intermarriage of the children of the marriage with the scientific children unlikely, and also prevent the perhaps painful thought to younger parents, that children were being born other than those of the marriage by the same father at the same time.

It is certain that science will reveal other methods of obtaining the "life," but for the immediate establishment of the scientific system, it is best that married people should co-operate with the Eugenic Institute in this new reform. All the apparatus which is now in existence in the Eugenic Records Office in America for investigating family history, and procuring data so as to further eugenic marriages and race improvement, could be employed in discovering any defects in the family history of those who would contribute the "life," and a good tree must bring forth only good fruit.

It will be recognized that while consanguineous marriages are most unlikely to occur between the children of the marriage with the scientific children, perfect security from any such risk can be obtained by a system of certificate of consent obtained from the Institute. In order to safeguard the grandchildren of the same father, and vice versa, all scientific children would have to obtain permission from the Eugenic Institute to show that there is no impediment to their marriage on the ground of consanguinity.

This at first seems complicated, but let us remember the elaborate suggestion by Eugenists amounting to the almost permanent elimination of love and contract, that a man should not marry the girl he desires unless family history, ancient and modern, physical characteristics and general health, showed the prospective bride to be entirely satisfactory from a eugenic point of view. <u>We hope that certificates for all marriages will be the custom then.</u>

The testing of the "life" at the Institute and of its pervious history, will have the watchful eye of the man of science whose task of saving and prolonging life will have added to it, the sacredness of promoting its inception, and of assuring its freedom from disease.

The details of the scheme of Celibate Motherhood, all of which safeguard the prospective mother and the children, are very important, and they have the one object of securing to the mother, her status in the community, and the certainty that her child will be legitimate. Residence in the Institute during pregnancy will be welcomed by them for the sake of assuring to their children, the hall-mark of the Institute and the record of the birth there.

The question of a generous fund for such a motherhood will find no carping critics in view of the splendid advantage that will be ensured to the nation, and of the admiration that will be felt for so unselfish a maternity. The proposal is that the State shall provide these mothers with an income for life in order that they many have the entire control and rearing of their little ones.

It will be readily seen that by the time the eugenic child is old enough to begin to earn for itself, its mother will be too old to take up again the work she had relinquished when she decided to have a child, or indeed to work at all, because probably it will be only women from twenty-five to forty years of age who will choose this path, and if 15 years of caring for and rearing her child, or children (should she desire to have more than one) is added on to her age, she might well be cared for by the State for which she has done so much.

The endowment of motherhood should form one of the most important objects of the future. Instead of spending thousands of pounds on emigration that may bring to our shores undesirable citizens, how much better it would be to support a proposal, which, from its economic standpoint, is entirely reproductive from beginning to end, which is certain to bring about race improvement, and help to solve the problem which faces us and which must be faced.

CHAPTER SIX

An Experimental Honeymoon

Editor's note: A Southern society girl (Marion) and a starving artist (Walter) agree to live together in New York City; she becomes his model. However, if the arrangement is discovered by her aristocratic family, it could lead to her disinheritance. On the other hand, if she married, and subsequently divorced him, this could also lead to her disinheritance. Since both individuals have had previous unhappy relationships, they are leery of marriage. They vacillate as to whether or not they should break the co-habitation arrangement. The characters are based upon Sinclair, Meta, and Craig. Sinclair expresses his feelings about being trapped in his first marriage, and the ambivalence of wanting to marry a woman he thought more compatible to his lifestyle. It was probably written during 1912 when he was living with Craig in Holland. Only one complete copy of the fifty-page manuscript was found. Pages eleven and twelve were removed by Sinclair and were not found elsewhere. Two additional folders with scraps of this story were also found.

("A second Marriage is the triumph of Hope over Experience.")
Dr. Samuel Johnson

Marion Bradford came softly down the stairs of the bungalow carrying a candle and peering over its flickering blaze with a queer smile on her face. She wore a pale blue silk kimono, blue bed-room slippers, and her long golden hair was loose on her shoulders. She was tall, rather thin, and bore herself with a girlish dignity — though she was to be twenty-five her next birthday. At least Walter Mathews thought she was about that age. Perhaps she was a little older. He was not sure. Her large brown eyes were usually sad, but there was often a certain expression of humor in them, a

---

"Experimental Honeymoon" Sinclair Manuscripts, Series III, Writings, Unidentified, Lilly Library, Indiana University, Bloomington, IN.

part of the brave smile that curved her lips, into habitual sweetness. At times she looked as young as twenty, and fragile and gracefully pretty. At others, when she was tired, she looked thirty or more — and the habitual smile was then unmistakably forced. It was the smile of the blasé society girl.

"Oh, is that you?" she asked now as she reached the foot of the stairs and held the candle aside so that she could look at the man in the low chair by the library table in the room beyond. "I thought there were strange influences abroad."

"Yes," he answered, looking up at her without changing his attitude of lounging ease. There was no light in the library, except the dim one that reached into the room from the hall where Marion stood with the candle. Evidently he had been sitting there in the dark until the moment before when the moon had slipped in at the windows.

"What did you come back for?" she asked, taking a few steps toward him and pausing.

"What did you come down for?" he counter-questioned.

"I was cold and couldn't sleep. I want some hot milk. Shall I heat some for you?" she asked, moving on thru a door at the rear of the hall.

"Yes," he answered, as she went down the passageway leading to the kitchens.

When she came back to him a few minutes later with a steaming sauce-pan and two cups in her hands, he had not changed his position. He sat with his legs sprawled out in front of him, his head leaning against the tilting back of the Morris chair. She poured two cups of milk and handed him one of them.

Then, cup in hand, she walked over to the window and looked out into the moonlight and silence of the Florida pine woods.

"Come and sit down, won't you?" the man said.

"Speak softly," she said, "your mother is a poor sleeper."

"What did you come back for?" she asked again, as she returned to him and seated herself on the opposite side of the book-strewn table.

"I was just thinking," he answered, in a solemn voice, "just wondering —?" He sipped the milk slowly.

"I hope they were pleasant thoughts," she smiled over her cup.

He continued to drink the hot milk slowly.

He was a young man, perhaps thirty-two or three, blonde, rather delicate in appearance, tho his skin was clear and healthy and his blue eyes clean and straight forward. She noted the slight lines on his high forehead, the troubled, weary look at the corners of his mouth. She did not think he was handsome, yet she could not tell why. But she liked his appearance — it was unusual and distinguished. The rather massive head, the corresponding large, [*sic*] the clear cut features of his face were quite obviously those of a scholar, a man of culture and refinement. His perfectly developed and graceful body was that of a faun. This combination of the scholar and the wild, woodland thing made her feel that he should have been a poet instead of a painter — a painter of conventionally beautiful women. But artists of all kinds were a new type to her, so she was not able to make fine distinction in their characteristics. She found them all absorbingly interesting and worth her attention.

She was wondering now what remarkable thing this one was going to bring forth. She felt that some thing unusual was going to happen. She had felt it before she came down the stairs — in fact this psychic premonition had impelled her to come.

She silently watched him now. Drinking her second cup of milk and waiting for him to speak.

At last he laid down his cup, leaned forward with his arms on the table and smiled. "Marion, I was just wondering whether I should fall in love with you or not." He stopped.

"Well really!" she exclaimed. This <u>was</u> remarkable!

He continued to smile, evidently waiting for her to take up the subject, to help him on with it.

She laughed.

"How perfectly funny!" she said. "How funny you are!" Her voice was a bit tremulous, but he never noticed such things as that. He was too simple and direct, and always absorbed in direct results. He took no note of side lights or small signs.

"What do you mean?" he asked in candid puzzlement. "What do you mean by that?"

She was smiling mischievously now for she was really much amused.

"How very funny!" she repeated.

"What do you think of the idea?" he persisted, still straightforward, but slightly embarrassed at her continued laughter.

"Why, I think it is very interesting," she said.

She arose and walked across to the wide window-seat and sat down among its cushions. The light from the candle where she had set it in the hall did not reach that secluded bay window.

"Come over here," she said. "Let us talk about it."

He came and sat in a rocking chair in front of her. He did not sit beside her on the window-seat as any other man would have done. It was so like him to hold himself aloof, even in this moment of—yes, she would have to call it love-making—a queer kind, but that was what it was, she knew. She had experience in such matters, and she was enjoying the unique way he went about it. No man she had ever known before—even men who were not half as serious and as uncertain about their own state of mind as this one was,—would ever have admitted that he was <u>considering</u> falling in love with her! She was accustomed to men, who if they did not abjectly worship her, pretended at least that they did. But she had never heard a genius make love before.

She laughed again. But her laughter was not all amusement. It was partly intentional, to conceal a deeper emotion and partly to puzzle and evade him. For tho she was going to lead him on, was probably going to help him to decide positively that he was in love with her, she wanted time to think, to be sure that she wanted him to love her. She wanted time to analyze her feeling for him. How much of it was love, in the accepted meaning of the word, and how much was pity for his loneliness, a kind of maternal brooding over his unhappiness? She admired him intensely.

She knew he had the tenderest [*sic*] heart in the world—he had shown that in his married life. She admired his passionate love of humanity and his desire to benefit it; she knew his was the martyr spirit that would die with a smile on his lips if he knew that by dying he would bring relief to the oppressed. And because she knew his soul was dedicated to the pursuit of beauty she could not endure to see his energies wasted by unhappiness. She could not see him in a difficult situation without tears in her eyes. For with all his greatness of intellect, he seemed to her at times like a sweet, pitiful child, blindfolded and blundering through the thorn hedges of a commercial world.

But she now laughed to gain time. What do you mean?" he asked again.

"I mean that—that I think it is a very interesting idea. I am surprised, of course. What do <u>you</u> think of it?"

He considered gravely, before he answered.

"You have suffered as I have," he said. "Mother has told me of that early love affair — that was terrible, Marion. Why did you never tell me of it?" But he did not wait for her answer. "And of course you know my married life was very unhappy." His face was full of lines of pain now, tho he tried to smile. "I do not know which is worse — to have had one's dreams shattered before marriage, as yours were, or to have suffered in the way I did. At any rate, we both are veterans."

His voice had become very tender. "I hate to see such a fine girl as you wasting her life. I need love, companionship — I cannot picture living my life without a woman's love and you."

"Again she laughed, that low tremulous laughter that was close to tears. But he was only bewildered by it. He stopped abruptly, started at her, then asked: "What is the matter?"

"Forgive me," she said gently. "I can't help being amused at you — you are so honest and straightforward. But I am thinking seriously about what you are saying. Perhaps it would not be a wise thing for you to do. I am so ignorant, you know, so uneducated. I have never read anything but a few light novels — and I read them hurriedly, between dressing for a dance or dinner-party, or in some languid hour after too much bridge and too many callers. I went to a fashionable boarding school — but that doesn't count for education. You know everything, are interested in everything, — in all kinds of important things of which I know nothing. You understand music — while I have heard only the strain of a waltz or a two-step while I was being made love to on the ballroom floor. I've been to the opera, but I paid no attention, — some man was always at my elbow, telling me how beautiful I was, how he loved me. I really know nothing but love-making."

"I know," he said. "But you can learn. I could educate you. You have been interested in the things I've talked of to you — you are clever and quick, and are not satisfied with the life you've been living."

"I've hated it!" she exclaimed passionately.

"So, that is why I thought - - - You say that you want to do things that are worth while, to take part in some of the vital movements of the time."

"Yes," she said, as he paused, "that is true. But I am afraid we are sitting up too late."

She rose and started toward the door.

"But, Marion, I can't sleep. I went to my room and something impelled me to come back here. Two o'clock, I saw by my watch, but I find you awake. What were you thinking?"

"We will talk about that to-morrow. Your mother might be disturbed. Mrs. St. John Mathews is a conventional minded lady, though she is your mother, and I am entirely too gracious a guest to trample upon the ideas of my hostess."

"But I wish you would tell me something of what you think to-night. I am unhappy...."

She paused in the doorway, "I think, Walter dear," she said, "that you are very foolish to be considering new bonds after what you have just escaped from."

She lifted the candle from the table and went toward the stairs. As she began to ascent, she smiled at him over the candle flame. "Good-night," she said softly. It was a very sweet voice and a very sweet smile, he thought. Indeed, she was a very sweet girl — surely there was some bond of deep sympathy and understanding between them. He watched her graceful figure until she disappeared on the landing above. Then he arose — lighted the student's lamp on the library table, went over to an easel in the corner of the room, and lifting the drapery, stared at the picture.

"It is no good," he said to himself. "It shows that the artist was working without inspiration."

The lines of unhappiness deepened in his face. What a mess a woman could make of a man's life! he thought. His work had been going steadily downward now for years.

Walter Mathews had been married at the age of twenty-two. While a student of art in Paris, he had met a beautiful American girl who had given him inspiration for a picture. The posing had begun, and at the next salon, all the world was talking of Walter Mathews and his wonderful picture of an Ursuline nun. A month later the famous young artist was married to his model and was making the unhappy discovery that a beautiful woman with the face of an Ursuline nun might turn out to be a Zantippe — and with modern improvements.

After ten years of pain and disharmony between them, she had died; and he, having loved her through it all, was grief-stricken at her loss. For six months now, since that event, he had been sad and discontented. And here, after all this tragedy, he was contemplating new bonds. Perhaps he was foolish, as Marion had said.

But what was he to do? He could not work as it was. Thru habit, and because of those stingy shreds of marital happiness which Fate had occasionally doled out to him in the past, he learned to need the companionship of woman. Was it not possible for a man and woman to live happily together? Had it been his fault, as his wife had insisted? Did a man have to pay for love with his soul's life? Was it not possible for life and love to exist together, each adding to the fullness and beauty of the other, instead of thwarting one or the other? He went out under the stars to ponder the problem.

He always felt at peace and at ease with Marion. Life with her would be serene and secure at least. But was that enough. When there had been love, it had not brought him happiness. For he had been in love with his wife. She had thrilled him and fascinated him always, even while she tormented him. But Marion stirred him in no such way. There had never been any mad, fierce crying out of him being for her. Her mind was undeveloped in the ways he desired; so she did not seize upon his intellect and hold it to hers with sympathy and understanding. He felt no swift throbbing of his blood at the sight of her.

He had painted a half-dozen pictures since his wife had died. Most of those were portraits of her from memory — gruesome things that expressed the distortions she had wrought in his soul. He had tried to re-produce her in the beauty he had first seen in her, — and he had put into it the ugliness of what late years had brought. Then he had tried to portray her as the spirit of Discontent — but this picture also had been confused by the uncertainty as to what she really had meant to him. These distortions had been spurned by critics and dealers, and his bank-account had dwindled to a notice of "Overdrawn" — a name strangely appropriate to the work by which it should have been replenished!

What a terrible tragedy it had been! And now suppose he should fall into a new trap! The rides haunted him — why couldn't men and women try it for a while and find out? How could they be sure otherwise what they would mean to each other!

It was dawn when he returned to the house. Instead of going to bed he put on his bathing suit and went down to the beach.

Behold, there on the white sands sat Marion, also in a bathing suit, with a steamer rug wrapped around her knees.

"Well!" he exclaimed in surprise. "What does this mean?" He came up and stood looking down at her.

"Get the skiff and take me for a row," she said, quietly.

He obeyed without further questioning. When she was seated in the stern with her rug tucked carefully around her, he began to row out toward the islands, pulling with long, slow strokes. Neither of them spoke for nearly an hour. He rowed on, skirting a large island and drawing in to a cove on a smaller one just as the sun rose.

"Shall we land here and go into the surf on the ocean side?" he asked, breaking the long silence.

"If you like," she answered.

He ran the boat into the beach, tied it to a stake, and held out his hand to her as she stepped toward him from seat to seat. Her hand was cold as he clasped it.

"We will go straight in, and after a battle with the waves, I think your circulation will be better. You aren't as strong as you should be Marion. I must take you in hand and make you exercise more."

He looked at her pale cheeks, noted the usual smile hovering around her lips, and a wave of tenderness surged through him.

"What a fine, courageous woman you are!" he exclaimed. "I have never heard you complain. And I know how unhappy you've been."

"I'm not unhappy now," she said.

"You have taught me that life is full of splendid opportunity for usefulness and beauty. Before this summer, I lived for nothing but the empty social game."

They came out now on the ocean side. "Oh, how splendid the breakers are!" she cried. He caught her by the hand and ran with her, half dragging her as she held back, shuddering at the cold spray.

When they came out the sand was already warm under the semitropical sun. They sat down in it, and Walter said, "Now, let us talk."

Marion did not answer for several moments, then she said, "Tell me, why did you never got a divorce from your wife?

"I suppose I should have," he said in a low voice, "but whenever I talked of separation, it upset her so, made her so unhappy: She could not endure to live alone. So, what could I do? Besides, I always blamed myself. You see, I am possessed of that strange devil — called genius — or at least, I think I am, and it is all the same thing. Whether I have it or only think

I have. It affects one the same way. It throws one into moods — terrible moods, which will not permit the intrusion of any outside considerations, not even those that are dearest and most vital to one's soul. It makes one seems indifferent and cold, to a woman, at any rate. At least it made <u>her</u> unhappy. She could never understand that I loved her just the same at such times — it was only that my mind had to concentrate itself upon my work. So it was natural that she should seek happiness elsewhere, if I failed to make her happy. In fact, I taught her that she had that right. I taught her that a woman should be as free to seek love and happiness as a man. But she could not be happy with me or without me. I wanted to end it many times — but she was the mother of my child."

"The Radical Man and his mate!" exclaimed Marion. "No wonder it frightens the old-fashioned ones! The Radical Man teaches Woman new ideas and ideals, tells her she is free to live her own life — tell her in beautiful, idealistic terms. She takes him at his word, and seeks her 'freedom' — freedom from domestic cares, from the duties of motherhood, freedom to seek love wherever she pleases. And he has equipped her with beautiful names for all this. She learns his fine phrase and used them to bend him to her selfish whims! He has given her weapons she never had before; and with these she keeps all the old ones, too — those of the 'clinging vine.' She appeals to him as 'Wife' and 'Mother,' pleads her inability to stand without his support, moral and economic. What an equipment for a creature that has been in semi-slavery for Centuries!"

There was mockery in her voice, but there was pity also and her face was sad as she went on. "Marriage upon the old basis was wrong, of course. We can all see that, and we can understand why. But this much vaunted Modern Marriage upon terms of Equality — why should it fail. We really wonder why <u>it</u> should!"

He was listening now with intense interest. How well she understood! How clearly she read the problem that had kept him groping and puzzling so long! After all, it took a woman to understand another woman.

"But how can a man see all of that?" he asked, rather pitifully. "Of course, it's all clear enough now, since you explain it. And it's interesting, too," he added with a new note in his voice, his mind suddenly busy with the intellectual side of the matter. "Yes, it's very interesting as a stage in the evolution — or the emancipation — of Woman. I suppose it's a necessary stage. But — he looked up at her with an odd mixture of hope and doubt. "You would not be like that, Marion?"

"Ah," she said, "maybe not. At least, I would feel differently about your Art. It seems to me that a woman might love a man's Art as well as she loved him — as the soul of him, I should say. At any rate, she might be willing to step aside at times in order that so great a thing might have its chance — I know at least that I should feel that way about it. Nature has given me no special gift or talent. She <u>has</u> endowed you — and if I could help you to develop a great endowment, to fulfill a great purpose, it would make me happy indeed. It would mean growth for us both. If would be something nobler, broader in its benefit to the world, than the mere personal love of you for me and me for you. It would be a splendid thing between us, upon which our love would be more securely based."

He had been listening to her, eagerly. This question of his genius had been the great obstacle in his consideration of their possible marriage. As she finished, he said: "Then, Marion, I see no reason why you and I should not make each other happy."

He hesitated a moment, then went on: — "I must be honest with you, you know. I care for you deeply, but —" He paused and looked at her questioningly.

"Go on," she told him. "I want to know everything."

"I hope you will understand," he said. "I am not sure myself what it means. You are so dear — so lovely, you are all the things I most admire. But I do not feel about you as I did about <u>her</u>. I can hardly explain what the difference is, or why it is. There may be some quality lacking between us. Or it may be that I was so absorbed in her when I first met you — it is a thing that happens at first sight, they say — this swift, indefinable attraction. Or perhaps that was all burned out of me long ago. Tho after all, I'm not sure that it was the right way — that blind, seething, unreasonable passion which is called love. Love should be the result of reason. I believe I should love you more and more as time went by, in a way that is probably the only real way. Should I have told you this?"

"Why, certainly," she answered. "And it is worth considering. But I am not sure I believe in the importance of the thing you miss. I rather think it is some kind of delusion — has something to do with the old idea of the 'mystery' of the opposing, the lure of 'the unattainable.' Whatever it is, I have noticed that it often vanished after its object is attained — after marriage. And I have seen people marry without it and learn to love each other devotedly."

"At any rate, I have had my share of it. I have had enough of such devotion — or emotion — from men who called me 'Goddess' and 'Angel' and 'Miracle'— who swore they would die for one kiss! It has never appealed to me, except that once, long ago, when I was very young. Certainly it is not the thing I should want from you. I could have it from you if I wished it — if I waited and schemed for it. I know how to get it." She lifted her head and challenged him with proud lovely eyes to [display] her skill. "I might lead you on, keep you on tenterhooks with my coquettish tricks that I learned in the world, arousing you, evading you, fanning your passion until it was a consuming flame — until you were blind and mad again! But I don't want you that way. I would choose a more eligible man from the worldly viewpoint, if that were the thing I desired. You mean something better to me. You mean development and interest. My mind was going to seed before you took me in hand. You make me think and study. You mean growth to me — and you have taught me to prize growth."

Her cheeks were flaming, her eyes shining; and he looked at her and thought she was beautiful.

"If I want you at all, it will be because we know and understand each other, faults,— weaknesses and all — and we are sure we could bring each other the things that would really count."

She stopped and gazed out at the sea. Ah, how beautiful and desirable she seemed to him at the moment! But there was an aloofness about her; despite all that she had said, and he kept his voice calm as he asked, "Then why should we hesitate, Marion?"

"Because — you know yourself that the bonds are hard to break when once they have been bound upon us. Marriage is a serious matter, under the most favorable circumstances. I look around me and see all my friends, old and young, and — I don't believe I know one really happy couple. I am afraid of it — that's all. I am no longer a young creature, ready to jump blindly into a thing I know to be so full of pitfalls — pitfalls from which there is no escape except by the payment of a bitter price. Even when two people agree amicably to set each other free, the laws are strict. One or the other must be accused of some wickedness or crime; there must be lying and deception. No, it is not a thing to enter into lightly. I am afraid of it."

"Ah!" said the man. "So you feel that way too! I hardly expected it of you. It is natural that I should. Yes, marriage is a problem — one of the great problems that confront the men and women of this age."

His voice dropped to the meditative key. He was falling into abstraction, as was his way.

He continued: "Some one must find out about it. It seems to me that here is only one way."

He was thinking of himself and her, quite objectively as two highly involved human beings, intellectually and spiritually, facing a problem that concerned the whole human race.

"Someone must be brave enough to set the example; some one must make the experiment. And who could be more fitted than you and I? Neither of us would abuse the privilege. We both believe that marriage upon the old terms is an outgrown institution; it was a necessity of its time, to protect the mother and the child. But times have changed. Modern men and women know how to avoid having children until they are prepared to take care of them. Women are learning to stand upon their own feet economically, and to refuse — we must admit that some of them do — to be supported by men who do not love them or whom they don't love. Men and women are learning to love according to the dictates of their souls, instead of by economic necessity or legal force. If they can be depended upon to deal fairly with each other voluntarily in the relations of love, then they should refuse to be coerced. Surely no lover should wish to hold another when the other wished to be free!"

He was so absorbed now in his argument that he had lost sight entirely of the personal viewpoint. He was always able to stop in the midst of his emotions to analyze them.

"And so," he continued, "the thing to do is to make the experiment. As the world is to-day, it would not be permitted; but we could keep our secret until we had found out what we meant to each other. And then, if we wished it, we could be married according to their forms and ceremonies. Then we could proclaim openly what we had done, and why we had done it. Of course we would have to face disapproval and scorn, but there would be some who would know we had been right. If they refused to buy my pictures because they did not approve of my conduct, I would not care. I can always earn enough for simple necessities, and you and I would be willing to sacrifice the luxuries for the sake of what we believe is right. If your father found out, he would disinherit you — but he need not know until we have proclaimed it, and then I should wish to care for you in the best way I could."

He stopped and looked at her, wondering what she would think of this interesting idea. As he watched the strange expression on that sweet, high-bred face, it dawned upon him how all this might sound to a conventionally trained society girl. In his abstract consideration of a vital problem he had entirely forgotten her!

He had always been a radical. He had read Ellen Kay and Havelock Ellis and Edward Carpenter. But what could she know of such modern things? She had heard of scandals — of the intrigues of fast society men and women. But he knew that she had held herself aloof from these things, avoiding even the appearance of evil. He had heard her called a prude by her men friends. Besides, these intrigues of the social whorls were as different from what he was considering as daylight from darkness. But that was just the point — would she understand the differences? Those were things done in shame, with doubt and shame in the hearts of the doers. This other would be done in the open — at least, as far as the law would allow. Certainly it would be proclaimed openly afterwards, and with pride in the consciousness that it had been a sane, and beautiful thing to do. But would she be able to see it in that light?

He saw that she was agitated. The color came and went swiftly in her cheeks and she was breathing quickly. Suddenly be became terrified. Would she utterly misunderstand him? Would she think of him as a villain of the conventional sort? If so, she might never forgive him!

But even while he tortured himself with the idea, he heard a little sob and saw her sway toward him. An instant latter her head was leaning upon his shoulder. "I love you," she whispered.

"Marion!" he gasped; and repeated, "Marion!" Instinctively he caught her in his arms; and he felt the trembling of her form.

He was dazed. "Surely you cannot mean it!" he exclaimed.

"I love you!" she answered. "Did you not know it?"

"I never dreamed it!" he said. "I cannot believe it." He realized with dismay how unprepared he was for this decision — how abstractly he had been discussing the question with her.

"You dear boy, how could any one help loving you!"

"I can't believe it!" he said again; but even as he spoke, her emotion communicated itself to him. He pressed her tightly. "You lovely, lovely woman!" he exclaimed. "You trust me!"

"As I never dreamed I could trust a man," she replied.

Yes, she had faith. She believed in him and in what he had been saying; and she loved him! He was dazed, stunned. He was thrilled at the beauty of her conduct, at the simplicity and naturalness of her abandon.

But as he held her and kissed her, a fear clutched at his heart. What had he done? He had taken this sweet, old-fashioned girl and converted her to his wild, new ideas! Of course, he knew in his soul that it was an ideal thing, but — how would it work out? She would go on loving him, more and more — and before he knew just what she meant to him. And she would cling to him blindly — this clinging instinct that was deeply rooted in the feminine nature! Ah, God, he could not stand it! He had had all he could stand of it in the past.

He continued to hold her in his arms and to kiss her, but he felt that even now his kisses were cold on her lips. Would she not feel it too? In the future, if he should not learn to love her as he ought, would she not find it out and be miserable? That thought was torture to him, for he loved her too well to be able to endure her unhappiness.

So a thousand doubts and fears assailed him. But suddenly about the tumult in his soul, he heard her calm, sweet voice saying: "Some Frenchman had said that the eternal question of the man is, 'Do I love her?' While that of the women is, 'Does he love me?'"

"Why, she is reading my mind already!" he whispered to himself.

CHAPTER II
TRIED OUT

It was six weeks since the moonlit night in August when Walter Mathews had first proposed to Marion Bradford the amusing idea of falling in love with her. On a cold evening in October he stood with her before a rear window in a dingy little apartment in New York City. His arm was about her and they were gazing out into the murky strip of daylight in the narrow court between the two tall, shabby apartment houses.

"Yes, now we can make each other as miserable as we please," he was saying solemnly. They were a solemn looking couple.

She said nothing to his remark, and he went on: "You know, dear, we have got to make a success of this affair. We simply must. We must not fail!"

"We are going to be happy," said Marion brightly. But there was a wistful note in her voice. She agreed with him in what he was saying, but — the phrasing of his first sentence was not exactly as <u>she</u> would have preferred it. However, it was his way. He was saying what he thought, without wasting time to consider how lugubrious it might sound to her. He was honest and direct; he valued time and saved it in all ways that he could. Also, he had told her that he never meant to conceal a thought or mood from her, and she had hoped he would not. She could always be sure of how he felt,— that was something any woman should be glad of. She would never have to watch him or trap him. If another woman should ever come into his life, he would tell her frankly; just as he had told her that he still loved the memory of his dead wife, and sometimes suffered keenly about her.

He went on talking in the same solemn voice:

"They would hold us together if they could, whether we like it or not,— even if it should be destruction to one or both of us. But we will not hesitate to dissolve it, without tragedy, if we find that it is not for the happiness and best development of both of us."

He seemed to be half questioning her, and she wished he would not do that.

"Why, certainly, dearest." She answered cheerfully. "Both of us agree that it is an experiment."

"I would not injure you for the world," he persisted, earnestly. "Are you sure that if we decided that we were not making each other happy — would it pain you too much to —"

"The idea!" she protested.

But there was pain in her heart now, for why must he dwell so insistently upon the idea of failure, upon the fear that she might suffer thru a separation more than he?

Also, she knew that it <u>would</u> hurt her terribly to give him up now! He had come to mean so much to her during these days while she was planning to become his — wife, should she say? Or — during these last days of her — girlhood. She smiled as she hesitated over the phrases.

But was it possible, after all, that marriage must contain an element of permanence? If they had been married by law would the possibility of separation be so continually in his mind? Did the despised vows mean something in spite of their conviction that only what was in their own souls and the agreement between themselves — the facts of their union — really counted? Was not their present relation sacred in their hearts? Certainly it was in hers. But men might be different. They might need to be bound by laws.

But she would not want to hold him if she should find that he wanted to go. But she wished he would not speak as if there could be no doubt of her satisfaction and happiness with him if only he could manage to be happy with her. She knew, however, that this was his honesty and simplicity, his straightforward way of facing first of all the possibilities of failure in any situation. He had had a bitter experience once!

He drew her to him and kissed her.

"You are the finest, truest, loveliest girl on earth!" he exclaimed, and then a minute later, turning abruptly from her and starting across the room, he said: "But we are losing time. Let us have supper and then we will work on the picture. Do you feel equal to posing to-night?"

He was uncovering the easel — which had been unpacked the hour of their arrival — for a look at the unfinished picture.

She spoke lightly, saying: "Of course I do." But she followed his movements with wistful eyes. How preoccupied he was!

He had forgotten her already. His mind was all on the picture. "We are wasting time!" he had just said, while they talked of their life together. But they had already discussed these things and agreed upon them, she told herself, so why should they keep on discussing them?

"Our first meal in our own home!" she exclaimed gaily, following him as he went to the tiny, dingy kitchen. She rolled up her sleeves and set to work at once. He helped her in all that she did, for they had no servant and he would not permit her to serve him.

"And I'm going to make you happy," he exclaimed, while he was setting the table. "I may be a genius — though there is a great division of opinion on that question." He smiled humorously. "I may or I may not be a genius, but I _am_ a man. And I'm going to make you happy. You are the bravest girl in the world!"

"I am not afraid," she answered him.

"Where did you put those paper napkins?" he asked, looking about for them. "No laundry bills for table linen in this house! And after to-night we will have paper plates — the kind they use in bakery shops. No dish-washing, either!"

They got the supper ready, she cooking the meat, and he setting the bread and fruit and nuts on the dining-room table and while they ate, he talked on. "Half the unhappiness of life is due to the waste of time and energy spent in the preparation of elaborate cooked meals. If one has a servant to do these things for him, there is still the worry of overlooking the servant. You are going to read books, while other women are peeling potatoes and making mayonnaise and washing dishes."

"How many beautiful and interesting things we are going to do!" she exclaimed. She knew that he had learned all of these things in his effort to solve the problem of domesticity with his former wife. What a cruel thing his life had been! She had risen from her chair to get something, and in a sudden fit of pity and tenderness she threw her arms around him "Poor, dear boy!" she exclaimed; and at the same time knocked his elbow, causing him to drop his fork with a piece of chicken on it to the floor.

"Oh!" he exclaimed. "What is the matter?"

Of course, he had not known what was in her mind, and he was asking for information. So his voice held none of the tenderness that was impelling in her. It seemed cold and annoyed.

"I'm sorry," she faltered, hastily releasing him and stooping to pick up the fork.

"That's all right," he answered, quietly. "But what was the matter?" He had reached for the fork too, and had gotten it. "Do not ever pick up things for me," he said, in a calm practical voice.

She felt ready for tears now. But she controlled herself and returned to her chair. This was the "coldness" that his other wife complained of. It <u>was</u> rather disconcerting!

"What was the matter, dear?" he asked again; this time there was a note of softness.

"Oh, I was just thinking how shamefully you had been treated by fate." She was struggling to keep her voice steady, and to accept calmly these trifling peculiarities of manner. He was not impulsive or demonstrative — that was all. He acted upon his reason — and he did not understand actions in others prompted by emotion. That was simple enough. She rebuked herself for her sensitiveness. She was as silly and sentimental as the rest of them! She would not let herself be like that!

"Now listen, dearest," he was saying, calmly, as if nothing had happened. "To-morrow I want you to begin to read some books I've got for you. You will be meeting my friends soon, and you must know something of the things they will talk of. Also you must read some good novels.

"Yes," said Marion. She was mistress of herself by now and was amused again at this strange, unloverlike [*sic*] lover. At least he was different from all her pre-conceived notions of husbands. But as she discovered each new characteristic which made him so different, she realized that back of each was common-sense and a keen appreciation of the value of useful and beautiful ways of spending life. There was never any futility or pettiness, but always something constructive. She had learned so much from him already; and now in this intimate association with him she was going to get a broader, nobler vision of life.

New and undreamed of possibilities were coming to her every hour. He had ideas — oh, how full of ideas that dear head of his was! Life with him was hope and promise, adventure and progress. How different from the old conventional rut! How wonderful to find ways to avoid so many of the troubles and trials that she had once believed to be unavoidable, and ways to introduce in this place lovely and serviceable things of the soul. How could any woman have failed to appreciate the chance to live, and work, and grow with him! What if he did have faults — they could be forgiven for there were enough rare virtues to out-number a multitude of so-called faults.

She wanted to jump up again to kiss him. But she thought better of this. She would leave <u>him</u> to make such advance in the future. Not that she felt any trace of resentment, for she had accepted his recent conduct as his way. But it was the thing she had been taught — to let man make such advances. Suddenly however, she was seized with an adventurous spirit, a curiosity to know how he would behave; this "gambling" spirit, as she called it, forced her to act against her old training. So, making sure that his fork was out of danger, she went cautiously, and bend over his shoulder, and laid her cheek softly to his. "I love you" she whispered.

He turned in his chair and put his arm around her, and held up his face to be kissed. "You are so good and sweet!" he said gently "I must make you happy."

"Why do you say <u>must</u>?" she asked. "Do you not know that you cannot fail? I love you for what you <u>are</u>— not for what you may do to please me."

"Do you feel that?" he asked.

"I can't give you as much as you can give me," she replied. "I seem to have the best of the bargain. But I will try not to let it be so."

"Marion, you almost make me unhappy when you talk like that. You are the most unselfish, the bravest, the most beautiful soul I ever knew. I am a terrible old dragon — when I am busy with my picture-painting. Suppose I should make you suffer? It would be a sin I would rather die than commit!

They cleared away the supper things, and afterwards, he read to her for an hour. Something about German Art — but she was not listening. She could not stop thinking about him — about them, about this strange adventure. He was interested in what he was reading, and she was vaguely wondering how he could be so absorbed in that. — It was their wedding day! Then she took herself in hand again. Was she actually letting herself feel hurt because he was not spending all his time telling her that he loved her, that she was pretty, and noble, and 'this and that'? That was the way that ordinary women made mountains out of molehills — molehills that at last grew into mountains.

She frowned at herself and began to listen — but only as he was finishing the article. So, when he asked her what she thought of it, she did not know what to say.

"Were you not listening?" he asked, in a voice that reminded her of a once dreaded school-master. She stared at him, just as she used to stare in girlhood.

His face softened, his eyes grew humorous. "What were you thinking of, dear?" he asked gently.

"You," she said, in a relieved tone.

He had forgotten her again. His eyes were thoughtful, and lines had come into his forehead and around his mouth, grim, set lines of preoccupation. She arouse with a sinking heart, and went to her room to put on the gauzy evening gown — a souvenir now of past glory — in which he was painting her as "The Coquette." He had said that she would forget the "challenging smile" and the "alluring eyes" after she had lived with him for awhile. She had been an artist in the use of them once, and such perfection, — even of wickedness — should be preserved.

"You are not smiling!" he exclaimed, soon after she had taken her pose. "You look like a child that has just been spanked. Cheer up, for Heavens sakes!" His voice was coldly disapproving.

She bit her lips and tried to imagine herself in a ballroom, chatting with some admiring swain. "There, that's better!" exclaimed Walter, in a relieved voice. And without any word of thanks to her, he began to paint busily.

For an hour he worked silently, with only "Chins bit higher, please" or "You _must_ keep your eyes open!" He might have been painting from a plaster cast, such were the cool, critical glances he bestowed on her!

At last her head began to swim, and after she had stood that as long as she could she sank down on the couch back of her. She thought she was going to faint, but she tried to smile at him, to keep him from being frightened.

"Oh, I was just getting it right," he said, reproachfully. "Are you tired?"

"I'll be all right in a moment," she said, trying to conceal her feeling.

"Don't try it unless you are equal to it," he said absently, and he began to paint from memory.

Presently, without looking at her, as he went on with his work, he said, "I can do without you now. Go and lie down."

She got up and went to her room, feeling that she had been dismissed from the schoolroom because of misconduct or failure to know her lessons. She threw herself on the bed. "Oh, oh, oh!" she sobbed, with her face in the pillow. "Oh, oh, oh!"

If only he would come and kiss her! Surely he would. She raised herself slightly and listened. There was no sound from the room beyond. "Oh, oh, oh!"

No, she would not have his kisses! He evidently considered her a mere appendage to his important career, a necessity in certain moods, an alien in others. Oh, the selfish brute!

After all, he _was_ a brute!

Why, she was only a convenience to him. When he could spare the time — how did he dare to take her love so lightly! Was it because it had been given so freely? Was it true that man must be forced to pursuit? Must women coquette, hold aloof, torture him with doubt and uncertainty, to make him appreciate her love when she gave it? Yes, this talk of men and women dealing fairly and openly in the relations of love was very fine in theory, but when it came to actually living these carefully considered theories, man was a selfish tyrant! He could not appreciate a straightforward, honest surrender. He must be snared, and then held by force of law, or at least by the artifices of the sex-game. Here she had given herself as frankly and unreservedly as this man had — and he was accepting her gift as unconcernedly as he took a glass of water. It was possible even that he did not respect — Oh, no, she knew better than that! He was too fine for that, she said. The trouble was simply that he was an egotist who took her love as a matter of course!

And to think of her here in this hideous little flat with him when she might have been comfortable in one of her father's elegant homes, driving her own electric, ordering servants about! To think of all the proud, gallant, light-hearted gentlemen who would so gladly be hovering around her, calling her "goddess," "princess," "adored one!" He had never called her anything more endearing than "dearest." Ungrateful, self-centered, impertinent — always talking of the danger of not being able to love her enough!

At least she was free to go. That was a comforting thought. All she had to do was to tell him kindly but firmly that she was going back to her father. There would be no trouble of a divorce, no false accusations. She was glad that she would not have to accuse him of some wrong against her, and to convict him before the world. That would have injured him forever, perhaps. It might have ruined his chances for the success of his Art. And if he should wish to marry again — she drew in her breath sharply. Would he wish to marry some other woman? Well, if he did she should certainly not want to hold him! Indeed, she was going to give him his freedom now.

Yes, she would rise up in all her dignity and tell him, quietly but haughtily that he need not worry about <u>her</u>! She would go home and marry one of those gallant, adoring lovers, and she would have her own servants and she would —

What would she do? Go to dinners and talk of the races, the last fashions, the latest recipe for mixing champagne punch? And then, when her gay, successful worldly husband had drank too much of that champagne, he would kneel at her feet and tell her how beautiful she was, how she adorned his home, how he only asked of her to always be well dressed and beautiful and gracious. So life would go on, and endless round of dinners and automobiles and theater parties. At least she would be called beautiful names.

Suddenly she caught her breath and listened. He was putting up his paint boxes! She heard the tin lids click, and then she heard him going to the tiny bathroom to clean his palette and brushes. When he came to her she would be cold and distant and proud. She would not let him see her suffer. She sprang up to powder her nose to conceal the tear-stain.

"Marion!" he called, exactly as if nothing terrible had happened. "Come, look at the picture."

"Very well," she answered, in a voice as calm and indifferent as she could make it, "In a moment —"

She smoothed out the crumpled ball-gown, brushed back her disheveled hair, and applied some more powder. Then she drew herself up and walked into the sitting-room, erect, proud and self-possessed, and very, very cold! He was standing before the easel, looking at it with smiling satisfaction. He reached out and took her hand without glancing at her. He cried, his eyes on the canvas. "Isn't it great! It's the first good work I've done in years. And it's all because I've been able to put my mind on it, instead of being distracted with fears and doubts about — someone else. Instead of having to stop to reassure you that I love you." He pressed her hand. "I've been able to give myself up to inspiration, sure of myself and of you, sure of your interest and sympathy."

He still gazed happily at the canvas.

"See how beautiful you are!" he exclaimed. "Don't you admire yourself?" He smiled at her now; but without letting his glance linger upon her long enough to notice her haughty mien he turned back to the picture.

"Quite charming," She said, in uncertain tones. She was staring at the picture, in genuine wonder. There, faintly outlined was her old self, her radiant, girlish self, — long vanished save in the memory of those who had known her then; for time, and thought and a "social life" had left lines and hollows in her face with the passing of years. But the artist had supplied the soft contours and tints of extreme youth. He had caught the essence of her "alluring coquette smile." the world would probably say that the woman portrayed there was beautiful. But oh, how repellant it was to her! Now she knew all the meaning of that smile, all its selfish, unlovely appeal. And he had been the one who had taught her to understand it. He had talked to her of beautiful things, and he had set her an

126

example of beautiful, useful life, so that vacuous, selfish face there was hideous to her. She glanced at him furtively. He had known what he was doing! He had done it with a purpose! There had been a lesson to teach!

His thoughts seemed to be following hers. He was saying: "It isn't half as lovely as you are now — tho the world might think differently. The next picture is to be of you as you now are — the serious, purposeful, unselfish woman, living life instead of posing, — a pretty, self-centered doll! And the third picture — ah, how can I describe it. I see it clearly in my mind. I've seen the look on your face often when I was sad and you tried to comfort me — that brooding, protecting, mother-look! Ah, what a lesson the three pictures will teach to this vain, folly-ridden world!"

He turned to her now, and put his arms around her and held her off from him while he looked into her eyes. "You are helping me to do these things. You brave, lovely woman! My sweet — what shall I call you, Marion" I have never been able to find the right name for you. The ordinary love terms are so inadequate. Nothing seems to express what you mean to me. You are my Hope over Experience! My Star of Hope! — that is what I shall call you!"

Suddenly she buried her face in her hands.

Oh, my dear, dear one!" she cried. "I am not worthy of such a man! I do not deserve you. No, I do not! I have been misunderstanding," — she was sobbing now with her head on his shoulder — "I've been thinking horrid things of you, losing my vision of you, I am weak and petty, I do not deserve to stay with you. I've been miserable —"

He interrupted her, saying in a voice that was almost comic in its utter dejection, "Miserable! So I've made you miserable already! Ah, yes, I might have known it. I am not fit to make any woman happy. And I was feeling so hopeful, so satisfied. You seemed to me the promise of all I had longed for. But I've always feared it — marriage. It is an impossible thing" — He was falling into abstraction, as he usually did. "Yes, marriage is a bridle with a curb bit — two bridles with curb-bits. But I thought that if you could stand it, I could."

She burst out laughing at this. How absurd that he should always say something of this kind: "He could stand it if she could!"

He was puzzled as much by her laughter but those tears — they must be accounted for first. "Tell me just what you've been thinking, Marian?" he asked, gravely.

She took his hands with a gay little gesture, she looked at him with the old humorous smile.

"I've not been thinking at all, dear. That was just the trouble. Something swept me away. But it is over now; it is a great thing, that habit you have of analyzing emotions. Half the troubles of life come from failure to do that."

She paused to consider, a little frown of thought on her brow. After a moment, she said:

"There must be some deeply rooted instinct in women that impels her to resent anything that might interfere with her hold upon a man's attention. See! I do not want you to spend all your time kneeling at my feet paying tribute to me. And yet when you failed to do it, I was miserable!"

She took a step nearer to him and laid her hands on his shoulders.

"Dear, I have had my first convulsion of adjustment—and my reason has conquered! Here's a pledge for the Future, to the dominance of Reason over Love." She kissed him on the brow.

He caught her to him, murmuring, "My triumph of Hope and Experience."

*　*　*

One morning, a month later, Marian awoke and found that Walter had gone out while she was still sleeping. There was nothing unusual about this; he often arose without disturbing her. But this morning the discovery of his absence brought a thrill of anxiety with it. They had been so happy of late—almost too happy for it to last, so the wise ones of this world would have told her.

She had begun to believe during the last few weeks that nothing—unless it were death—could ever interfere now with the fullness and perfection of her joy. She was working hard at the course of study Walter had laid out for her—she was learning German and French, reading all kinds of serious, thoughtful books of which she had never even heard before he got them for her. She was getting well and strong again, under the health regime he prescribed for her—and the joy of love and interesting work.

She loved him now, fully and completely, she knew, and he had shown every indication of a devotion as deep as her own. She was greatly amused sometimes at his utter dependence upon her! He could not budge without her! If he went out for a walk, if he went just to the corner to post a letter, he invited her to go with him. He called upon her for advice in every little matter of business — and she must always be near, even when she was not posing, when he was at work on his pictures. He did all these things with the same pre-occupied air, in the same manner of abstractions that had upset her so once — on the first day of their life together. But this had never disturbed her again — how could it when once she had accepted it as the right way, and when he showed in every other way his desire for her interest and companionship?

This morning she lay there in her tiny bed-room, thinking of all of these things and wondering what gave her this new feeling of apprehension. Was she going to get the habit of moods from him? She got out of bed and threw on a kimono and went to look for him. She would make sure at once that there was no reason for this foreboding.

She found him sitting dejectedly by a window in the dining-room, staring before him at the falling snow. Marion approached him softly and going back of his chair, bent down and kissed him on the cheek.

"Morning, honey-boy," she said using the Southern love name he liked.

He drew slightly away from her and looked intently in her face. After a moment he said:

"Sit over there, Morning Star, I want to talk to you."

His voice was a gloomy as his look.

She obeyed him. Seated on the couch in front of him, she questioned him calmly with her eyes.

"I've been having a terrible time with myself," he said moodily.

"What is wrong?" she asked.

"I'm afraid it has been a mistake," he said.

"What has?" she asked.

"I love you very dearly, Marian, you know that, don't you?"

"Yes," she said.

"You mean more to me every hour," he continued. "But then comes that old restlessness and dissatisfaction. I don't know how to tell you about it."

The harassed expression of his face stirred her with a longing to help him. "Tell me," she said gently.

"It seems to me that I am not getting my work done — that I never can get it done! I do not know what to do about it."

"You surprise me," she said. "Isn't that picture good?"

"Yes, that is good," he admitted.

"Well, then, ought that not content you?"

"Nothing contents an artist," he replied. "It only serves to waken old memories in my soul — to make me think of the things I wanted to do and haven't done. It seems to me as if I'd have to go alone, bury myself somewhere, and never think of anything but the work I haven't done and that I must do. I let myself be tempted — I sink into happiness and contentment. Don't you see, dear? I long for love — for the things that other men desire — but it seems to me that I've no right to them. I have no time for them. And above all, I have no right to ask a woman to stand my moods of discontent." He stopped and looked at her anxiously.

"I understand," she said quietly.

"Sometimes I shall need you terribly," he went on. "I shall hate myself and call myself a fool for having let you go. I shall long for you —"

She interrupted him, asking quietly:

"And you do not think I would be satisfied to stay with you, to keep out or your way when you do not need me, to be there when you do? You have brought me only good so far," she went on. "Every hour with you is a lesson to me. You mean development and interest and joy to me. You make me think and study and learn. You teach me patiently, and — in short, I could not live with you or near you with out being benefited. If that were not so, I am not sure I'd be willing to stay, — even tho you needed me." She paused and waited for him to speak.

"I am filled with despair, this morning, Marion. I belong to my work — I must not run any risk of hurting it again."

He was speaking as if trying to defend himself from some impending invasion.

She rose quietly to her feet.

"Very well, dear," she said. "I understand. And I would not want to interfere in any way, let me get the breakfast this morning, and afterwards I will get my things packed. I will go back to my Aunts, so that you can come to see me when you are lonely. Do not have any reproaches for yourself. I do not feel one bit worse for this — this beautiful experiment."

"Is that really true, dear?" He asked wondering. "It has been good for me in every way," she declared. "It has made me realize more thoroughly that life is not a set and finished thing — that we must go on with it, experiment with it, evolve and progress. This has been a step in the right direction. I am satisfied and grateful to you for it all. Now smile, and get yourself in mood for breakfast." She walked toward the door. "We are good friends still — better friends than ever," she added as she passed out of the room.

She went back to her bed-room and dressed. Then she went to the kitchen. As she was getting the knives and forks out of the box, he came and put his arms around her.

"Star of Hope," he said softly, "You are never to leave me again! Never, not even for a day! I do not believe I could live another hour if you were not with me. Morning Star, promise me that you will never go again."

She laughed as she turned and accepted his kisses.

"You dear, funny old thing! I haven't gone anywhere yet. And didn't you know all the time that I wasn't going?"

He looked to her like a forlorn little boy who had been left in the dark room alone and was so glad to get back to his mother and the light.

"Marion, I want to tell you something," he said. "There was the time once, soon after you and I decided to try this experiment, when I asked myself if a consciousness of permanence — that 'for better or for worse' idea with its suggestion that the worst was to be expected and endured — was not necessary for the establishment of the right psychic attitude between two lovers. I put it aside at the time, with the decision that it should not be necessary but the answer came to me so forcibly just now. You will be interested to hear about it.

"I woke up this morning feeling deeply my love for you — how dear you had become! I arose and dressed and went into the sitting-room, expecting to do some good work in this fine exhilaration of mind. I began to think that the time had come when we should settle our affairs — there was no need for longer delay. We were as happy together, as congenial in all ways as anyone could wish to be. I began to think of marriage. Marriage by law, I mean and instantly that old fear swept down on me. I was like a wild horse with his feet in a tangle of wire. I was at the mercy of that terror, that horror of being caught and bound. I felt like kicking frantically to be free. You see, I was carried away by an instinct, just as you were once. My reason had just been telling me that we were happy. But that old instinct drove all else from my mind."

She laughed. "It would seem the New Man as well as the New Woman, will have to overcome some superstitions!"

PART III

Search for Health

The fast is to me the key to eternal youth, the secret of perfect and permanent health.— Upton Sinclair, *Fasting Cure*, 1911

CHAPTER SEVEN

The Health Hunters:
A Farce Comedy in Four Acts

Editor's note: This sketch is a proposal for a theatrical production. It shows various health cures, crusades, and regimens of the early twentieth century that Sinclair liked to satirize. Many of the cures and Eastern spiritual traditions depicted in this proposed drama will be familiar to the present-day reader. The draft is 12 pages in length and only one copy was found. It was probably written around 1910-1911 when Sinclair was focused on diets and cures.

[ACT I]

The first act opens in a summer garden of a hotel in a small village in Connecticut. Mr. Jeremiah Sassingham, original discoverer of the "Sassingham Perpetual Suspender," has just arrived. Mr. Sassingham is an elderly gentleman, stout and rosy, a good-natured and lovable old body, a shrewd business man, but extremely gullible as regards all altruistic and cultural enterprises. He is in a state of perpetual agitation concerning his health, and is the prey of innumerable charlatans, who have plans for making him all over, and, incidentally, the rest of the world, too.

He has telegraphed for his favorite nephew, Dick Burroughs, a college boy, to come and help him in his latest emergency. Dick arrives, and learns that his uncle has come to this place, having heard wonders of the miracles that are being worked by the Hochheimer Hygeia Sanatorium (Naturopathic), presided over by the famous Dr. Gustavus Hochheimer.

"The Health Hunters: A Farce Comedy in Four Acts." Sinclair Manuscripts, Series III, Writings, Articles, Lilly Library, Indiana University, Bloomington, IN.

He tells his nephew about all the wonders of mud baths, air baths, cold water treatments, internal and external, the squirrel diet, bare-foot promenades, sleeping on the ground, and all the rest of the regimen. Dick is dubious, and reminds his uncle of numerous other fads which he has taken up, with no benefit — the milk diet, the sour milk diet, the meat diet, the spinach diet, homeopathy, osteopathy, and all the various baths, springs, hospitals, and sanatoriums which he has visited. He tells his uncle he never saw him looking better in his life, at which the other becomes highly indignant, and rattles off a terrifying catalogue of symptoms.

Mr. Sassingham also insists that his nephew looks terribly run down, and must come in and take the cure with him. He deplores the reckless life of the college youth, who does not take the trouble to weigh his food, pays no attention to the calorific content, and for all he knows may be in the incipient stages of elephantiasis or housemaid's knee. He insists that his nephew's anxiety to get back to college is probably due to some love escapade which he is carrying on. (The uncle is always attributing these motives to Dick, who is a very shy and embarrassed youth, and lives in deadly terror of the strange female personages whom he encounters while following in his uncle's train).

Dr. Hochheimer is introduced, clad after the fashion of the nature men, with long hair and beard, bare arms and legs, a very scanty pair of trousers, and a shirt which looks like a fish net. The Doctor is very anxious to have the distinguished Mr. Jeremiah Sassingham as one of his patients, and tells wonderful tales of his achievements, and manages to wriggle out of the dilemmas into which he is put by Dick's questions. The latter becomes more and more strenuous in his efforts to dissuade his uncle, until suddenly the Doctor happens to mention that among his patients is the rich widow, Mrs. Evelina Everson, whom Mr. Sassingham recognizes as an old acquaintance. Some mention is made of her charming niece, Miss Polly Lancaster, at which Dick manifests interest.

Mrs. Everson is summoned by telephone. She is an angular, imperious lady, who is undergoing the same adventures as Mr. Sassingham. Amid great awe she announces that she has fasted fourteen days and lost fourteen pounds, and in the subsequent treatment has gained twelve pounds. Dick, in some perplexity, inquires if one has to pay the same board while undergoing the fasting cure, and declares that he would like to run a boarding house on that basis. It is October, and Dick thinks it is rather late for outdoor treatments in the "altogether" but it is a bright sunshiny day, and he thinks he can stand it if the weather holds good. He listens to enraptured discourses by the doctor on the joys of playing bare-footed in the snow and sleeping in the tree-tops. However a single glance at Polly, who comes on shortly afterwards, is sufficient to remove Dick's last scruple, and he agrees to undertake any treatment that may be recommended.

He and Polly come to a private understanding, and agree that they will be able to make life tolerable for each other. Polly describes her agitation and dismay because of the habit of her aunt, who is an inveterate match-maker, and insists on finding her a husband in each new cult to which she becomes a devotee. At present she is being thrown into the arms of a young man who is trying to cure freckles by a diet of radishes and Brussels sprouts. Dick learns that one is allowed outside of the compound for a couple of hours during the afternoon, and there is another town near by, with a first class restaurant, and also an ice-cream saloon just around the corner.

ACT II

Act II takes place at six o'clock the following morning, and shows the men's outdoor air baths in the Hochheimer Hygeia Sanatorium (Naturopathic). Mr. Sassingham and his nephew have appeared on schedule time, but the weather has changed; it is cold and damp, and they stand shivering in their overcoats, hesitating to take the plunge, while meantime the devotees of the back-to-nature movement are disporting themselves around them, clad in sheets. We encounter a series of absurd types of health enthusiasts. One man is followed about by a small boy with a bucket of water and a dipper, he is absorbing a pint of water every fifteen minutes. Another man carries a little pailful of juice of carrots and turnips, and sings the virtues of the negative salts. Another man is wheeled, lying in a wooden frame, somewhat resembling a coffin, completely covered, except his eyes and nose, with a casting of mud — he is taking the earth cure.

Others tell of the delights of absorbing a pint of sand per day, and invite Dick to share in the joys of some raw vegetables and grains. Another makes a specialty of sterilized handshakes, and puts on a pair of paper gloves before he is introduced. Another man climbs about in the trees overhead, and from this vantage point proclaims the joy of returning to the primitive habits of our arboreal ancestors. Another pounds himself upon his hairy chest, and proclaims his likeness to the chimpanzee in the forest. A stout and florid-looking individual is introduced who is taking the fasting cure for obesity. He has now fasted thirty-seven days, and to the perplexity of every one, has not lost a pound. While the attention of the spectators is diverted elsewhere, he is observed to take the carcass of a chicken out from underneath his sheet, and gnaw surreptitiously upon it. Other fasters appear in various stages of emaciation.

A wild uproar is heard, and a man rushes across the scene clad in flesh colored tights, except for a very small pair of trunks. He is waving his arms and bellowing in agony; about him is cast a very fine net with heavy black dots, giving an effect of a swarm of bees — he is taking the bee-sting cure for rheumatism.

The sound of rushing and splashing water is heard. Just off stage some of the enthusiasts are treating themselves to hot and cold percussion douches, ice baths, fomentations, salt glows, etc., and they emerge in various stages of exultation and agitation. Meantime Prof. Hochheimer and a furiously athletic looking assistant explains the various remedies. A few flakes of snow come sifting down; Mr. Sassingham and his nephew conclude to postpone their initiation until later in the morning. The patients retire and the visitors' hour is announced.

Some of the lady patients come on and an extremely lean and terrifying personage corners Dick, and tells him that she is taking a thirty day fast for the conquest of soul power, and among other things she has found out how to get control of the white corpuscles in her blood, so that she can slay all hostile germs. Dick is finally rescued by his uncle, who takes him to task for his unscrupulous lovemaking.

Mrs. Everson appears, with Polly, assiduously attended by the young man who is trying to cure freckles and apparently so far has not met with much success. Polly confides to Dick that her aunt has been closeted the greater part of the night with a new kind of health specialist, a professor of the art of mind-cure who has made her ashamed of all the practices of the Hochheimer Hygeia Sanatorium (Naturopathic), because they are so grossly material, based upon the body and its desires. Mrs. Everson has been suddenly smitten with a realization of the supremacy of her subconscious personality, and she is determined to return to New York and place herself in the hands of Prof. Marmaduke McGregor, of the McGregor Institute of Metaphysical Mechano-Therapy.

There is an excited discussion concerning all these matters. Mr. Sassingham is bewildered, but insists upon his symptoms, and declares that he must take at least a few days of the squirrel diet, in order to be assured of his mastery of his carnal nature. Mrs. Everson declares her intention to concentrate all her thought-powers upon him, in order that he may join her at the college of mind culture.

Dick and Polly arrange it between them that he is to doctor his uncle's squirrel diet in some amusing fashion, which will be certain to disgust the old gentleman with the nature cure in a very short while. Polly expresses the opinion that the old gentleman is afraid of the wrath of Dr. Hochheimer, and Dick thinks that perhaps if he gives that gentleman a good punching, he may be able to afford additional demonstration of the superiority of the carnivorous diet.

ACT III

Act III opens in the parlor of the Metaphysical Institute of Mechano-Therapy. The professor and his wife are giving an afternoon tea, to which the devotees of innumerable psychic cults are invited, to meet the rich Mrs. Everson and her beautiful niece. There are specimens of the many varieties of New Thought cults; there are the Koreshites, who teach that the world is a hollow sphere, on the inside of which we live, and that the believers of Koresh shall be the one hundred and forty-four thousands saints who will be caught up into Heaven; there are Soul Communists and New Adamites, Professors of Chiropractic, magnetic healing, telepathy and hypnotism, palmistry and spiritualism. A stout lady explains to Mrs. Everson the "Wisdom of the Illuminati," and a learned gentleman with spectacles sets forth to Polly the Laws of Self-Prolongation, whereby one may avoid those evil thought conditions which have shortened human life from eight hundred years in the days of Noah to eighty years at present.

Mrs. Everson is greatly thrilled by the discourse of a follower of Francis Schlatter, the new Messiah and teacher of the "natural tone." He explains that every human being is pitched in a certain musical key, and the discovery of this key is the secret of success in life. It becomes plain to Mrs. Everson that she has at last found the correct way of selecting a husband for Polly, and the conversation becomes embarrassingly intimate. It is interrupted, however, by a theosophist, who tells of the wonders of

Karma, and exhibits the paraphernalia of mysticism, as they are set forth in Madame Blavatsky's "Secret Doctrine" and "Isis Unveiled." He tells of a wonderful society of re-incarnation which is holding its sessions just around the corner, and is bringing to bear the thought waves of many millions of people simultaneously upon the achievement of their purposes.

Mrs. Everson is so much excited by all this that the Professor takes alarm, particularly as he see that Polly is fascinated by this latest phenomenon. What pleases Polly is the fact that this new doctrine teaches that marriage is only of the soul, and consequently she sees an opportunity to escape from the clutch of the gentleman who sits beside her, devoting himself throughout the conversation to determining the musical tone of her personality. (This, however, she does not explain until later on). McGregor is called aside by his assistant, Prof. Zimmelini, who has received a telegram from some one he has employed in the Hochheimer Sanatorium, announcing that Mr. Sassingham and his nephew are on their way to the McGregor Institute. Prof. McGregor at once comes forward, with the dramatic announcement that he has received a telepathic communication; though waves impinging upon him to make certain the immediate approach of Mr. Sassingham. Amid great excitement, he proceeds to diatribe upon this marvelous power of his, and builds up a climax. The bell rings, and he lifts his hands announcing the advent of the new disciple. When the door opens, a stout Irishwoman, with a scrub-bucket in her hand, demands "Will yez be afther wanting any scrubbing done this afternoon?" A little later, however, the bell rings again, and the Professor again works up his climax, and amid great triumph the old gentleman and his nephew come in.

The guests now take their departure, and Mr. Sassingham's case is taken up. It is diagnosed as a "sympathetic inhibition of the sub-conscious ganglia," and it is decided that hypnotism is the remedy. Mr. Sassingham is hypnotized, a la Sevengali, and proceeds to go through some diverting antics. The professor sets forth that he himself does not know the meaning of what his patient is doing; that the whole matter is in the control of certain super-terrestrial personalities who were acquainted with him in some of his pervious re-incarnations. Presently Mr. Sassingham is found to be in the midst of composing an epic poem on the subject of "Vivisection," whereupon all agree in discovering marvelous mediumistic powers in him, and it is decided to hold a séance, in order to give the higher forces an opportunity to set forth their recommendations as to his future career.

140

A messenger appears with a note from Prof. McGregor, which he finds to be a communication from Dr. Hochheimer, offering him one third of all that can be made out of the Sassingham family, provided that he will cause them to return to the Nature Cure Sanatorium. The Professors decided to do this. Meanwhile, however, Polly has an interview with Dick, in which she beseeches him to do what he can to persuade her aunt to join the Theosophists and become an adept in the doctrines and practices of the Yogis. Dick is perplexed that she should have become interested in this. She asks him to trust her, and so he says he will do what he can. She exclaims in terror that she is afraid it will turn out that she is pitched in the key of C, and will be betrothed to the disciple of Francis Schlatter.

The séance gets under way. Dick manages to conceal himself, and catches the Professor's assistant in the midst of a materialization, with all the usual accompaniment of white gauze, phosphorus, etc. This happens behind the cabinet, the inside of which is visible to the audience, but not to the participants in the séance. Dick gets the assistant by the throat, and declares that he will expose him and incidentally choke the life out of him, unless he delivers a message from the spirit controls, instructing both Mrs. Everson and his uncle to put themselves immediately in the hands of the Yogis. This message is duly delivered, to the great consternation of Prof. McGregor, who breaks up the séance in a wild rage.

ACT IV

Act IV opens in the parlors of the Brotherhood of the Inner Circle of Transcendental Theosophists, and here we have all the paraphernalia of this transplanted Hindoo mysticism. The people all wear yellow and scarlet robes, and move about with mysterious demeanors. A group of them are disclosed, sitting in a circle, and repeating the magic syllable "Om," transporting themselves into a state of Nirvana. Some tell strange tales about their experiences in previous re-incarnations and upon the excursions which their souls are accustomed to make, leaving their bodies and traveling to other planets and taking part in the ecstasies of the inhabitants of these.

We witness various others of the occult practices of the Yogis. One man is attaining a state of bliss by concentrating his attention on the seventh button of his waistcoat; another is developing soul power by drawing deep breaths and expelling the air in short explosive puffs. Yogi Babu Banana, who is the head of the sect, immediately attaches himself to Polly, who, however, submits to his ministrations, since she understand that the attentions of the adepts are purely Platonic. Dick finds himself in the grip of a sentimental stout lady, who tells him how she consecrates her life to the sick babies of the slums, by means of absent treatment. She immediately divines wonderful occult powers in Dick, and tells him that he must become a qnani — this is pronounced "nanny," and Dick says, "It seems to me that I am the wrong kind of a goat." Polly to become a "ehelah," while Mr. Sassingham is to become a "guru."

He explains to them the wonders which these Theosophists are going to work for him. The head Yogi wields tremendous spiritual power. He has some forty million followers in India, who all at a precise moment during the day place themselves under his control and concentrate their minds upon any purpose which he directs.

As usual, Mr. Sassingham interferes with Dick, rebuking him for his recklessness with women, and warning him that in these sacred portals only the most spiritual of thoughts must be permitted to enter. Dick casts a dubious eye upon the devoted attitude of the Yogi Babu Banana, who has Polly cornered on a sofa. In the end Polly rises abruptly and breaks away from the great master, and whispers to Dick in the deepest indignation that the man has been making love to her.

The two now realize that they are no more contented with Theosophy then with any of the other cults, and they resolve to make one desperate effort to tear their relatives out of the hands of all these charlatans. They concoct a scheme between them, and shortly afterwards Dick takes occasion to get into conversation with one of the adepts, and informs him that a great mistake has been made — that his uncle is not the rich Mr. Jeremiah Sassingham, inventor of the "Sassingham Perpetual Suspender," but a poor farmer from up the state. This news spreads swiftly about the room, and Mr. Sassingham suddenly finds himself the center of an icy frost. He has been given to understand that he can be the recipient of the benefits of all the innermost secrets of the cult without delay, whereas he now learns that it will be necessary for him to spend seventeen years in study before he can be a "guru," and that it will be necessary for him to start of with a forty day fast, in order to purge himself of all his animal attributes.

And then Polly, who is again pursued by Babu Banana, puts on a look of agonized misery, and tells him that she wishes him to apply his deepest thought power to help her in her distress. He listens with great interest and offers to bring all his powers to bear. Polly tells him that she had that morning a violent quarrel with her aunt, who has disinherited her and cast her off, and will have nothing to do with her. From that moment Polly finds no difficulty in escaping from the Yogi, who now proceeds to devote all his attentions to Mrs. Everson. He corners that lady upon the sofa, and sits holding her hand and explain to her the secrets of her seven concentrative auras, while in the meantime Mr. Sassingham, outraged and indignant, is watching from the other side of the room.

It has been becoming manifest through the play that Mr. Sassingham is in love with the widow, but he cannot get up the courage to declare himself, owing to that "Sympathetic inhibition of the sub-conscious ganglia." Now, however, he comes forward and stands behind Babu Banana's back, listening while the latter sets forth that Mrs. Everson can become a "Guru" in only a few weeks, and without any fasting at all; and he suddenly breaks [into a] wild rage, and denounces the whole miserable swindle, seizes the Yogi by the back of the neck, and throws him into a corner, declares himself to Mrs. Everson, and clasps her in his arms.

Dick and Polly retired to another room while this is going on. They are now summoned, and they listen in terror while Mrs. Everson announces to Polly that she has now definitely and finally made up her mind upon the subject of her soul state, and the proper marital destination of her niece. Polly, in terror, declares that she will not submit to her aunt's dictation, and Dick comes forward and backs her up. Mr. Sassingham is indignant at his nephew's presumption, and commands him to be silent. Dick refuses and there is a lively quarrel among the four, until finally the discovery is made that the purpose which Mrs. Everson has in mind for her niece is that she shall marry Dick forthwith. Whereupon they both capitulate, and the four bid a permanent farewell to occultism, and declare themselves for a beefsteak dinner without further ado.

CHAPTER EIGHT

Restore and Keep Your Health by Controlling Emotions

Editor's note: This four-page draft is a health education essay giving advice to control anger, fear, and anxiety in order to prevent disease. It is typical of many essays written by Sinclair from around 1910 through the early 1920s. However, some health information found in this essay is not accurate in view of health and medical knowledge, as we know it, in the early twenty-first century. It was likely written around 1920 and could have been originally planned for the Book of Life *(1921). Two drafts of this essay were found. In the drafts, "Health" is underlined in the title.*

We live in the Golden Age of Science. Our great scientists have made discoveries, have acquired knowledge, which if it were in our possession, would so greatly enrich our lives, so greatly increase our happiness and peace, that we would feel as if we had been born into a new world. For instance, if you <u>knew</u> that each time you became angry, or worried, or anxious, or afraid, you actually poisoned your body, and that in time the accumulation of poison in your body would give you cancer, or tuberculosis, or some other dreadful disease, would you not seek to avoid anger? Some of us have a dim idea that anger, and worry, and fear injure us, but not many of us realize the immediate and terrible effect it has upon the body. Many of us have observed that after a fit of anger we feel sick. We have a headache, or some other minor ailment. Or we feel stimulated — which is what we are, just as if we had taken a "drug." I have certainly had this experience, and I have seen children make themselves ill by a fit of temper.

"Restore and Keep Your Health by Controlling Emotions." Sinclair manuscripts, Series IV, Lilly Library, Indiana University, Bloomington, IN.

We are too apt to say to ourselves, "I would have had that headache, anyway. It is due to something else." Or, "I feel better after blowing up, getting it off my chest."

But scientists, including some of out most distinguished surgeons, experimenting in laboratories, have discovered that a very serious set of things happen to the <u>body</u>, immediately, in anger, or fear. For instance, the adrenal glands throw adrenin [*sic*] (a powerfully poisonous stimulant), into the blood in abnormal quantities. The liver throws sugar into the blood in large quantities, sometimes producing diabetes at once! The flow of gastric juice is completely arrested, in anger or fear, as is also the churning process of the stomach, which is necessary for digestion; these cause food fermentation, and this fermented food poisons the system, while the body has also been deprived of nourishment. All these things are very injurious to our bodies. They put a strain on the heart and on the blood vessels, as well as on the overtaxed glands and digestive organs. It has therefore been proven positively that we cause serious illness by anger.

Would it not be of much use to us to acquire more, and yet more, of such knowledge of this? One piece of knowledge which each of us should possess, and keep near the top of our minds for constant use, is that <u>we do not understand ourselves nor our fellow men</u>. If we understood ourselves, we would get along much better with ourselves. And if we understood our fellows, we would be far less apt to come in conflict with them.

Psychology now teaches that our subconscious minds are full of things of which our conscious minds have no knowledge. These things manage to get into conflicts with each other down in the depths of our subconscious minds, with the result that our whole organisms, both mental and physical, become utterly irresponsible! These conflicts in our subconscious minds cause us to do things which we ourselves do not understand. We deceive ourselves with the idea that we are doing certain things for a certain purpose, when in reality we are doing them for an entirely different purpose.

The child, for example, becomes angry with its parents. He is afraid of his parents and therefore does not try to have revenge on them, but his anger goes down into his subconscious mind and stays there; so he goes out, kicks a cat, or throws a rock into the window of a neighbor's house. Sometimes he goes out and does something much more serious, such as setting a house on fire. Often these acts of mischief are committed days,

146

months, even years after the fit of anger, and after the child has entirely forgotten it <u>in his conscious mind</u>. He has no idea that he is doing these things for revenge upon his parents. The psychologists call this kind of act "compensation." The "ego" having been opposed, "compensates" itself in a "perversion." We adults behave in the same perverted way, without knowing it. Obviously, we need to understand ourselves.

That is why our first study should be "human nature, or mind and body." We must have a better understanding of <u>ourselves</u>, first then of our fellow men, so that we will be able to get on better with ourselves and with our fellows. If we have no spiritual incentive, such as "brotherly love," <u>there is a selfish, purely material one which all of us will do well to heed</u>! This one incentive alone — the protecting of our bodies from physical disease — is sufficient. Once we become convinced that we suffer physically, that we bring disease upon ourselves, that we shorten our lives, by being angry, worried, or afraid, (<u>or even anxious</u>), we will learn gradually, if not quickly, to control our emotions.

Self-control is very difficult to acquire, especially late in life, when our habits have been formed. We have acquired the habit of giving way to "feelings." When we are angry, we <u>want</u> to be angry; we feel injured, and we desire to express our resentment. We enjoy boiling and seething mentally, against the other person. Some of us will deny this — we will declare that we do not enjoy being angry. But it is true that we do! I remember that I was quite shocked when some one told me I enjoyed a fit of temper. But I watched myself a while in anger, and found that it was true. I <u>wanted</u> to indulge in resentment and self-righteousness.

CHAPTER NINE

"Little Algernon" Fragments

Editor's note: The Health of Little Algernon *was a serialized novel published in* Physical Culture *from December 1911 through June 1912.* * *The drafts of this serial were originally titled, "Little Algernon." Similar to themes found in "The Health Hunters," this novelette satirizes popular health cures and belief systems of the Progressive Era. It also promotes Sinclair's own fasting cure. The two unpublished works did not have titles or installment numbers. I have entitled them "Miss Toots, the Spiritualist," and "Lois, the Eugenic Suffragette."†*

The protagonist of the novel, Little Algernon (Francis-Edward Puirbody), is an extremely rich child. He was orphaned at an early age, is sickly, and overprotected. He is told by his grandmother to avoid designing women who want to marry him for his money. As an adult he becomes involved in one treatment or belief system after another to cure his chronic stomach and other ailments. He wholeheartedly embraces each new regimen and gives away substantial funds to the designing women, and sometimes men, who ask him to support their health cures and causes. Finally, at the end of his misadventures, he becomes lost in the Canadian wilderness and undergoes an inadvertent fast. He gains health and stamina, meets and marries a country girl who is not interested in his money, and they presumably live happily ever after.

However, a possible darker ending to this novel was found among the unpublished drafts. What I have called "Lois, the Eugenic Suffragette" could possibly have been a gloomy final chapter to the novel. Among other sentiments it describes in detail the painful feelings of unrequited love. There are two complete copies and one partial draft of this 19-page installment. An additional four-page draft, which appears to be the last segment of this installment, ends at the bottom of a ragged page. No further pages or copies of this fragment have been located. Therefore, it is not known if this unpublished installment was, in fact, an alternative ending to the novel, or if more was written.

No correspondence has been found between Sinclair and Bernarr Macfadden, the publisher, to clarify why this, and other segments, were left out of the published serialized novel.

---

*"Health of Little Algernon, being the story of a twenty-million-dollar quest for health," Physical Culture, December 1911, January–June 1912, xxvi–xxvii [serialized novel].

†Both stories from, "Little Algernon," Sinclair Manuscripts, Series III, Writings, Articles, Lilly Library, Indiana University, Bloomington, IN.

We begin with the tale of Algernon's involvement with the Spiritualists. I am calling this story fragment "Miss Toots, the Spiritualist." It is found from page 4 through 13 of an unidentified draft. It appears to be part of a story found in installment III of the published serialized novel. It should be noted that names of characters throughout this satire often allude to their health cure or cause. "Toots" is a reference to a horn that toots to announce the manifestation of a spirit during a séance. Angelina refers to angel spirits; however, Angelina is anything but an angel.

"MISS TOOTS, THE SPIRITUALIST"

Algernon had got to the state where all doctors and all drugs and all diets were like a nightmare to him. He was ready to go and throw himself into the river in a frenzy of despair, instead of which he went and threw himself into a big leather arm chair in his club, and sat there, looking like a weeping Niobe in trousers.

Cheer up, Algernon, help is on the way! It happened to be ladies' day at the club. If Algernon had known it, he would have gone to some other club, but there he was in a chair brooding upon suicide, when there came a rustle of silk petticoats, and by his side there stood Miss Angelina Toots, the sister of Mr. Tallywell Toots, the gentleman who played so important a part in Algernon's early career. But be it understood that Algernon had never been told anything about Mr. Toots, and so he had no suspicion of the sister on that account. Besides, nothing could be a greater injustice than to form one's opinion of Miss Angelina's character from that of her brother. Mr. Tallywell Toots was cynical and wicked; Miss Angelina was a lady of soul and altogether lifted above mundane considerations. She was a lady of indeterminate age, but very young as to her costume. Her costume was of the very latest fashion, and it would not have been until you heard her speak that you would divine the unusualness of her aspirations. She stood looking at Algernon.

"Good afternoon," she said.

"Good afternoon," replied Algernon, but did not move from his position. From which Miss Angelina knew that he must be in a very desperate state indeed, for our friend was ordinarily the very soul of politeness.

She seated herself in a chair close beside him and gazed at him intensely. "You are suffering," she murmured.

Algernon did not look up. Yes, he was suffering, but he did not want any woman to know it.

"What is the matter?" asked Miss Angelina.

He shook his head, and murmured faintly something that she could not distinguish.

"Tell me!" she pleaded. "Permit me to help you!"

Algernon gave a gesture of despair. "I am sick of my life!" he moaned.

"Sick of your life!" echoed Miss Angelina. "And with all your opportunities!"

"Of what use are my opportunities to me?" cried out hero.

"Mr. Puirbody!" she exclaimed, and then added in a low voice, "Algernon! You are wrapped up in your own petty cares! You have forgotten the infinite presence, which hovers above you and which guides your life. Ask yourself, is not that true?"

Algernon answered, "What use is that Infinite Presence to me when I can't assimilate any food?"

"Oh," said Miss Angelina. "It's your stomach."

"No," said Algernon, "to be precise, it's my liver."

"Your liver!" exclaimed the other. "What could be more commonplace, worldly and material than you liver? To think that you permit that to wreck you spirits, to blight the infinite possibilities of a great nature like yours! To think that you, who might be in tune with the infinite —"

"Miss Toots," asked Algernon, "did you ever have anything the matter with your liver?"

The lady blushed slightly. The question was a somewhat delicate one. In the best society young ladies are not supposed to have livers. She leaned a little closer to him, and speaking a little more intensely, "I would give you some thought to cheer and encourage you, something that you can hold before you, to lift you out of the petty cares of the moment. What though this life be a vale of sorrows, what though you are compassed about by evils, which you cannot understand — think that some day you are to escape from all this! Infinity stretches before you, you have many worlds in which to live! Don't you realize that?"

"You mean that I'll have a better liver the next time?" he asked. He shook his head sadly, his faith was not equal to the effort. If it was not his liver, it would be some other part of his [body]. Never would he be well in this world or in any other world, and it was quite in vain that Miss Angelina pleaded with him, and sought to cheer him up.

Never in her life had she met so hopeless a pessimist. Nothing good had ever happened to him, nothing good ever could happen to him. She wrung her hands; the tears started into her eyes, tears of pity for the sad fate of a man who had so many blessings and so many possibilities, and could get no happiness whatever out of them! And all the while Algernon was sitting and watching her, and thinking to himself, "No, no, Miss Toots, it's no use at all — my grandmother warned me about those things!"

"But then you do not believe in immortality of the soul?" asked the young lady at last.

"Why — er — yes," said Algernon, "of course." Did he not teach it in Sunday School?

"Yes, I know," exclaimed Miss Toots, reading his thoughts. "You have repeated it as a formula all your life. But does the actual realization of it ever come to you? Is it faith that guides you in your daily life, that you are some day going to cast off this mortal body and fly away to higher spheres?"

Algernon was staring at her. Really now, when he came to think of it, that was a startling idea. Suppose you could know that. The other rushed on, pressing her advantage, "Suppose it could be something real, present to you at every minute of your life — ."

Algernon was starting at her. "How do you mean?"

There came a strange thrill into her voice. "The dead live," she whispered.

He stared.

"Yes," she went on, "They live. I know it. They live with me! They come to me, they speak to me, they tell me the secrets of the next world!"

"Miss Toots!" gasped our hero. This was a brand-new one, and he was caught in spite of himself.

"Come!" cried Miss Angelina, "give me an opportunity to prove it to you! Let me be the fortunate soul to unveil to you the wonders of the future world! Let me bring before you some of the great souls of the past, who will tell you all that you seek to know!"

There was an impressive pause. Then Miss Toots added, "They may even tell you what to do about your liver."

So Algernon capitulated. An appointment was made for that very evening at the home of Miss Toots, and Algernon went there and met the celebrated Madame Trovatore, the spiritualistic medium. They seated themselves about a table, and Madame Trovatore closed her eyes, and moaned and shuddered and wriggled and kicked, and pretty soon from underneath the table came strange mysterious raps. Each rap meant a letter, according to Miss Toots. She explained them with breathless excitement. "G-e-n-e-r —" "Not the General!" she exclaimed. Ah, you have come to us! Tell me, shall we have revelations tonight?"

"Yes," answered the General, and Miss Toots turned to out hero. "Whom will you speak to?"

Algernon was perplexed. This was rather sudden. "Why, I don't know," he said.

"Anyone you please!" exclaimed the other. "Think! Of all the great men of history whom would you prefer to know?"

"Why," stammered Algernon, "let me see. I guess [name left blank]."

"All right," said Miss Toots.

Madame Trovatore had seized the lead pencil and had begun to write upon a bit of paper before her. Miss Toots was leaning over her shoulder reading the scrawl.

"I am [name left blank]," she read. "What have you to say to me?"

She turned to Algernon. "The time has come!" she cried. "What would you know?"

Algernon hesitated. He had not been prepared for so sudden an introduction into the hereafter. "Why, really," he stammered.

"Speak," exclaimed Miss Toots, "the hour is passing."

"Why, ask him, shall I eat beefsteak or oatmeal?" said Algernon.

Miss Angelina asked the question very solemnly, and Algernon waited in breathless suspense while the pencil scratched over the paper. Letter by letter Miss Angelina spelled it out to him. "I lived on goat's milk." And then a sudden hush fell in the room. The two auditors stared at each other. Was this the revelation, the secret which Algernon had been seeking for so many years of suffering? Goat's milk! "What else?" asked Algernon, his heart in his throat.

"What else?" whispered Miss Toots.

"Nothing," wrote the pencil. There was a pause.

"Ask him something else," said Miss Toots.

Algernon pondered. All his life he had dreamed of Robinson Crusoe, and of the happiness of such a life. Robinson Crusoe was his ideal of human happiness. "Tell me," he murmured, "shall I ever be well and happy?"

Miss Toots repeated the question, and there came an answer that thrilled Algernon to the very depths of his soul. "Some day you will find my island."

Algernon was trembling with awe. There could be no doubt to him of the meaning of this cryptic utterance. "Some day you will find my island." Some day he would be well and strong and happy, like other people! His heart leaped up, he could have shouted for joy.

"What else?" Miss Toots inquired.

"Nothing," he said. The cup of his blessing was full.

"Who else will you speak to?" she inquired.

Algernon hesitated, and thought of who was there among the dead that had most impressed him in life. Ah, yes, he knew. "My grandmother," he answered.

"What is her name?"

"Vivian Styvesant Cholmondeley de Puyater."

Miss Toots repeated the name, and the pencil scrawled, "I am here! Speak!"

Algernon by this time had become convinced enough to speak to the medium himself. "Tell me, what shall I do?"

And the pencil wrote, "Trust Angelina!"

Algernon found himself trembling with awe. "But," he exclaimed, addressing his grandmother, and quite forgetting the presence of Miss Toots, "She is a woman."

The pencil scratched again. "Trust her," it said.

Algernon was almost beside himself in alarm. He could not believe that it was his grandmother, it did not sound like her. "Oh, give me some proof," he cried.

She will give you all," wrote the pencil. "She is one of us. The key to happiness is in her hands."

And so the séance came to an end. Algernon was left staring dumbfounded, with a mixture of awe and dismay. Deep within his soul something was crying out in rebellion against his grandmother's actions. She had no business to put him at Miss Toot's mercy like that; she ought to have told him herself. He did not like Miss Toots, he was afraid of her; she had too much soul for him. Also her toilets were too loud.

But he dared not disobey the oracle. He was hers to dispose of, and she carried him off to a place in the country, where spiritualists were holding a convention. And day after day and night after night Algernon attended séances. He learned to walk unterrified through the halls of death, he conversed with the spirits of [blank] and Aeneas, of Cl [sic] and Cleopatra and John the Baptist.

The country around was scoured, and three milch goats were discovered and imported for Algernon's especial benefit. Milk was not bad on the whole, but it became most desperately monotonous for him. He found that he could not drink very much of it at once without his stomach's rebelling; he would drink half a glass and then in a little while he would be hungry again, and he would have to go and drink some more. He found that he was an object of romantic interest among the spiritualists, when they learned that his diet had been prescribed by one of the great heroes of fictions. There was no longer any need for him to be ashamed; he carried his milk bottles around with him wherever he went, and drank before all the world.

Meantime he contributed a hundred thousand dollars toward the building of a new temple of spiritualism, and he understood the expenses of the publication of no less than seventeen great masterpieces on the subject of scientific research — masterpiece which reported the work of various celebrated mediums and professors whom he met at this conference — but meantime his terror of Miss Angelina increased day by day. It was she who had brought him to his convention, and she was the heroine of all his benefactions. She followed him about, she managed all his affairs, he could never get away from her, and he was in utter terror of her. He gave her thousands of dollars every day for various purposes, but the more he gave, the more causes there seemed to be left. At last he got into such a state of terror that he could not digest even half a glass of goat milk; he got into such a state that the mere thought of goat's milk filled him with nausea; and finally one night he pleaded illness, and while Miss Angelina was delivering a lecture on the coloration and conformation of the human aura, in cases of psycho-neurosis, he had his valet pack up his belongings and hired an automobile and fled to parts unknown.

It was not really as bold a venture as it seemed, for there at the convention of the spiritualists Algernon had met a new kind of doctor, and had at last learned all the secrets of his physical maladies. Dr. Pawnek was the name of this new doctor, and he was an osteopath. It was all wonderfully simple, as he had explained it. There were certain important nerves that ran out of your spine, and nature sometimes slipped up and didn't leave big enough holes for these nerves to get through, so Dr. Pawnek would lay you on your back and examine you, and after this he would know exactly which vertebrae were crocked, and exactly what bones had to be kneaded into shape. You stayed with him for a few months, and let him attend to you, and you went away a new man. Dr. Pawnek has slipped his card to Algernon at a moment when Miss Angelina happened to turn her back, and now Algernon was fleeing to his Sanitarium.

The continuation of this installment is found in the Physical Cultural *series.*

"Lois, the Eugenic Suffragette"

The next island at which the "Comet" arrived was Jamaica. They sailed into the harbor of Kingston, and Algernon was feeling a little better then, able to go on shore and take a stroll. One of the disadvantages of being worth forty million dollars was that Algernon never really had to do anything. When an ordinary human being on a yacht or any other kind of a vessel, arrives at a foreign port, he had his mail to get, and some odds and ends of shopping to do, and a whole lot of such ordinary human tasks; but Algernon's mail was got by his secretary, who answered most of it — he had only a few checks and legal documents to sign. All the purchasing was done by his steward or his valet. There was nothing for Algernon to do but to be rowed ashore and to stroll through the streets and gaze at all the busy and apparently interested people, and wonder why he alone among men should be forlorn and useless and friendless.

Algernon had been to Kingston before; he had been everywhere in the West Indies before, because that was always where they sent him when his lungs or his throat could not stand the winter blizzards. So there was nothing for him to see, there was nobody at home for whom he had to buy sea shells or picture postal cards. He was strolling along melancholy and restless, when suddenly his heart gave a leap. That man in white, who had just come out of a hotel and was stepping into a carriage — was not that Tommy Carter, his classmate in college? Algernon called to him, and he turned. Yes, it was Tommy Carter, and the girl who was sitting in the carriage and who turned also, that was Lois Carter, his sister, whom Algernon had met each spring when she came up to the college Commencements.

Well, well, they certainly were glad to see him, far more glad than they ever had been at college Commencements. It makes a great difference when one is far away from home and meets a friendly face.

Algernon was beaming with delight. He always had liked Tommy, and as for his sister, one could not use a familiar a word as "like" about such a girl as Lois Carter, one might as well talk about liking the Victory of Samothrace. It seemed a kind of mistake that she wore a sailor suit and was made of living flesh; she ought to have been cut in marble, with marble robes about her, standing on some high pedestal. At least that was the way Algernon had felt when he first laid eyes on her; he had stood there gazing at her, forgetting what he had to say, forgetting all about himself; and it had always been that way every time that he had seen her.

The Carters were poor — that is to say, they were poor according to the standards of the Puyster family. Her farther was a corporation lawyer, who got a fair salary, but not enough to count in New York. So Algernon should have been on his guard concerning the wonderful Lois. But he was spared all need for that by reason of the fact that Lois paid less attention to him than if he had been a sparrow hopping about on the ground at her feet. Algernon was not at all conceited; he did not think that he was anything especially remarkable, but he was used to having people treat him with deference because he owned forty million dollars, and he was always bewildered by the attitude of Lois Carter. He could have understood that she did not care a continental about his forty million dollars, but she was not even that. She seemed to be entirely unaware of his existence, so that sometimes Algernon was tempted to wonder if by chance her amiable mother could have failed to inform her that he had forty million dollars. It had been very humiliating and very tantalizing.

Up there at college there had been so many men that Algernon had been hopelessly lost, but now here he was in a place where there were no men, and she was actually glad to see him, and he had a yacht and she had no yacht, and he could invite her and her mother and her brother and take them to all sorts of delightful and interesting places. She should find that forty million dollars was something after all.

But alas for all Algernon's calculations! Lois said she did not care for yachting; at least, she did not care for sitting around on the deck of a vessel and being carried somewhere, half as much as she cared for getting a little sail boat of her own and taking it herself where she pleased. She did not care for automobiling; at least she did not care for it as much as she cared for getting a saddle horse and rambling about on the beaches or through the palm thickets and the trails that ran above on the hills of the island. Algernon found himself a guest instead of a host, and he found his forty million dollars of no more use than it had been in the college town. Miss Carter was as cordial and friendly as could be, but then she was cordial and friendly with the little native boy who brought the horses on which she rode, or with the old Negro fisherman who rented her a sail boat. There was something sublime and awe-inspiring about her untouched aloofness. More and more she seemed to Algernon like a goddess from the heights of Olympus, and more and more he found himself without any interest in the world except to follow her about and gaze at her and listen to her silvery laughter, and to the wild and wonderful ideas which poured in a continuous stream from her mind.

Algernon, you must understand, was an eminently respectable and conservative young gentleman. He had attended a Sunday school in one capacity or another all his life. He read his Bible each night and he said his prayers both night and morning, and he not only believed all that he read in the Bible, but he also believed in the gospel of the social proprieties and in the gospel of the old Knickerbocker families of New York.

And here was Lois Carter, who had been to college and also to a university, and who was preparing to study medicine, who was an ardent advocate of women suffrage and went out and delivered speeches from an automobile on street corners in the midst of Hell Kitchen; who believed in the emancipation of woman in general, and proposed to earn her own living and live her own life; who belonged to the Socialist party, and refused to stop talking when the police commanded her and was carried off to the police station like the veriest [sic] bomb throwing anarchist; and who not only was not ashamed of any of these dreadful things, but gloried in them all, and calmly informed Algernon that before she got through with him she would have him doing likewise!

She could not be deterred by any idea of social proprieties or even by quotations from the Bible. She gave Algernon dreadful books to read, and she talked about subjects which left him simply gasping for breath. Such was Miss Lois Carter, the newest example of new woman, a type that was altogether new to Algernon.

He was horrified to learn that there were many such and that there would be many more such as time went on.

Now whatever else one might say about Algernon, one had to admit that he was honest. It would have been very easy for him to win a small amount of regard from this imperious young lady by pretending to be a convert to her ideas, but Algernon was horrified by her ideas, and he was perfectly frank in admitting it. Miss Lois used to have a very happy time shocking him. Algernon was very much ashamed of himself because it was possible for him to associate with so very dangerous a character, but then on the other hand, Lois Carter was so obviously a lady and so obviously a goddess! There were times when Algernon wanted to fall on his knees and grasp her hand and apologize to her for his impertinence in daring to disapprove of her opinions.

Thus passed a couple of weeks of Algernon's life; I was about to say the happiest of his life, but I might go even farther to say the only happy ones of his life. Algernon noted a most amazing thing. That which all the doctors and drugs and sanitariums and treatments of two continents had failed to do for him was done by riding horseback and going sailing with Lois Carter; he was so happy, he was so preoccupied that he forgot all about his stomach, and all about his liver, and all about all the other problems of his health. He would have forgotten all about eating, had it not been for the fact that Lois had a very good appetite and he had to keep her company. He went about all day in a dream of bliss. It seemed to him as if he wanted nothing else in life than to ride horseback and go sailing with Lois Carter and listen to her silvery laughter and to the wild and wonderful ideas which poured in a continuous stream from her mind.

Did Lois Carter know about what was going on in the soul of Little Algernon? He did not know, he never stopped to think. For once the voice of his grandmother was completely silent in him. How preposterous seemed her counsels concerning the feminine sex when applied to a personage like Lois Carter, who so obviously had no earthly use for him, except to ride horseback with him and go sailing with him, and had no use whatever for his forty million dollars!

But, oh, the shocks and the agonies that came sometimes to the soul of our sensitive hero! Miss Lois had read thousands of books of which Algernon had never even heard. She apparently had taken all knowledge to be her province, and there was no subject about which she was willing to be ignorant; even the most dreadful of subjects, the subjects about which Algernon could not hear men talking without blushing and running away. Miss Lois was of the opinion that all young people ought to be informed on the subject of sex. She learned that Algernon had reached the age of twenty-five without being informed at all, and so she took him in hand and proceeded to tell him all that he ought to know, and this without in the least considering the fact that he did not want to know these things, and that he felt like falling overboard from the sailboat while she talked about them. She had actually studied the most dreadful and unmention-able diseases; she knew what caused them and she talked about them with the utmost serenity and insouciance, and yet with such simplicity and honesty as to make Algernon ashamed of his shame.

Also she had strange ideas on a strange subject which she called eugen-ics. She believed that just as men bred different kinds of horses and dogs for different purposes, and kept improving the breeds all the time, so ulti-mately they would learn to breed human beings and to [do] away with all the evil and misery there was upon the earth. And this was not merely a wild idea which Miss Lois was willing to talk about. It was an idea which she actually proposed to carry out in her own life. She made this statement quite casually and as a matter of course, and Algernon sat staring at her, his jaw fallen. He was not able to find any words to ask her what she meant. But a day or two later in another conversation he got an idea of what she meant. He happened to mention Bobby Symonds, who had been half back on the football team and also the prize debater of Algernon's class in col-lege. Since then he had become a lawyer and had been elected to Congress. He was [the] youngest member of the House and had a brilliant career before him. Algernon happened to mention his name, and Lois said, "Oh yes, I saw a great deal of him last summer. He is [a] splendid man. I asked him if he would like to marry me."

Then again Algernon stared, and again his jaw fell. There she sat, a goddess out of the skies, and with the utmost serenity and quite as a mat-ter of course, she said that she had asked Bobby Symonds if he would like to marry her! After a while Algernon managed to find his voice.

"How do you mean?," he asked.

"Why," she said, "I thought he would be the sort of man I wanted, and so I proposed that we find out."

"You — you proposed?" stammered Algernon.

160

"Of course," said Lois, with a smile. "When woman is free, she will do most of the proposing. Did you never think of that?"

No, Algernon had never thought of it.

"It is her affair in the main," added the other. "Don't you see? It doesn't cost the man very much."

Algernon sat pondering. "What did he say?" he asked at last.

"Oh, we talked it over," said Miss Carter. "There were some reasons why it wouldn't do. The principal one was his wife."

Algernon gasped, "His wife!"

"Yes," said Lois.

"You — you mean," stammered the other, but even stammering he could not get any farther.

"You see," the other explained, "he had married when he was very young, and wasn't happy. I thought he ought to get a divorce any way, but it seemed he couldn't make up his mind to it. He was superstitious, you know — like you."

It took Algernon several days to get over that entirely. It took him half a day to get to the point where he could bear to see Lois at all. He went off by himself and took a long ramble in the jungle; he had it out with himself there. He said his prayers and fought a desperate fight, but all in vain; he could not do without seeing her, even though he were to be damned and consigned to fire and brimstone for an eternity thereafter.

He went back and went for a sail with her that evening. And that evening the torrent of his pent up emotions broke loose. Try as he would, he could hold it back no longer. His pulses were leaping like mad, his head was swimming; there was a chocking in his throat. Suddenly, as he sat by the side upon the edge of the boat, his hand touched hers. He caught it; he fell upon his knees before her, burying his face and whispering, "Lois, Lois!"

She did not do any of the conventional things which the heroine of novels are accustomed to do in such an emergency. She sat very still, staring before her, and she left her hand in his.

"What is the matter?" she asked at last, her voice very low.

And Algernon, half whispering, half sobbing, answered, "I love you."

"I had no idea of that," she said at last.

And again there was silence. Algernon clung to her hand, and a fearful trembling seized him, so that he could not speak at all.

"I am sorry," she said, finally. "I am so sorry."

Algernon knew her well enough by that time, to understand what she meant. Her words were like a knell of doom to him.

"It's too bad," she went on after a while. "I thought we were just friends, and I thought we were having a good time."

Again there was a long silence. Finally Algernon whispered in a frightened voice, "You do not love me?"

"No," she said, "I do not love you."

"Not in the least?" he asked.

She answered, "Not in the least."

"Don't you think that you might ever love me, Lois?"

"No," she said, "I know that I could not. I should think that you would know it too."

Algernon knelt there, clinging to her hand, and pondered this. Why would he have known it? What did she mean? He could not think, and finally he asked her why.

"Ah, don't let's talk about that!" she exclaimed.

"I — I — don't understand you at all," he stammered. "You must explain to me. I must understand."

There was a pause. She hesitated how to say it. "When I marry a man," she said, "it will be because I have chosen him to be the father of my children. I must feel that he is the most perfect man that I can find for that purpose. Don't you realize that I could never think that about you?"

Algernon was crushed.

"Ah," she exclaimed, "I am so sorry. It seems so cruel to say! I know it is not your fault."

Algernon's voice trembled as he answered. "No, it is not my fault," he said; and he added, "It is something I have wondered about vaguely all my life, whose fault is it?

"It is a matter of heredity," Lois answered. "I don't know anything about your parents, I can't tell you, but somewhere there was a taint, and you are paying the price. That is no new idea; you can find that in your Bible. And she quoted, "For I the Lord thy God am a jealous God, visiting the iniquity of the fathers upon the children unto the third and fourth generation."

Algernon listened, and it seemed as if his blood turned cold within him.

"So that is it," he muttered.

"Don't you see," she said, "it is just because your parents before they married never asked themselves the questions which I am asking myself now? I am not thinking about myself, I am not thinking about you, I am thinking about the child."

The girl's voice had sunk low. Algernon looked up and saw that she was gazing at the stars above her. He bosom heaved and she stretched wide her arms.

"The perfect child!" she murmured.

There was a long silence. Algernon was awed and overcome. He let go her hand, he sat up, holding himself very stiff and straight. He had lost, but at least he would show himself a man. He fell below her standard in body, at least he would not fall below it in soul; he would not plead or complain. And he divined that for this she was grateful to him; she was very gentle, very tender. They sat and talked about other things, while the boat glided along through the starlit water, while the waves lapped softly against its side.

An hour must have passed before it suddenly flashed over Algernon that in all this conversation there had been not a word said, and apparently nothing thought about the one great thing which made the difference between him and the other men who might be in love with her — his money! He started when he thought of it; he sat for quite a while pondering the question. Ought he to mention it? Ought he to mention it now? He had always been haunted by the vague wonder if it might not be by some strange chance that Lois Carter did actually not know that he was the possessor of a million dollars. At last he made up his mind that he must allude to it, he could not be at peace until he knew her mind on that subject as on all others. He was sure she would not mind, she was so frank about every thing. He tried several times before he could get up the courage.

At last he said, "There is something I want to say to you."

"What is it?" she asked.

"I didn't — didn't — want to speak about my proposal again, but like you — you ought to know, you ought to think of this, Perhaps I have not so much physical power as other men, but I have power of another sort."

She smiled. How beautifully she understood things! Her mind was like a rainbow leaping vast spaces of thought.

"That power," she said, "does not depend upon my marrying you."

Algernon found that his own mind was stumbling in the valleys. It was necessary for her to lift him up to the heights where she dwelt.

"How do you mean?" he asked.

She answered, "You can give me all the money you please, you know."

"Algernon was on the heights now, and there was no touch of cynicism in his soul. He knew exactly what she meant. She always had that calm assurance that when he had read and studied he would believe as she believed. She would make a suffragist and a Socialist out of him, and then he might use his money for the cause.

"You see," she added, "even if I married you, I would not want to use it unless you believed in the cause as much as I. I have my own life and my own responsibilities; I would not take yours."

It was the last word they ever said about it. But as Algernon sat and gazed across the starlit water and pondered this, he made up his mind that he would pretend to believe in Lois Carter's causes, even if he really did not. Was not she a goddess, and was not he a poor worm beneath her feet, and how therefore would he decide what was right? How should he dare to set his judgment about hers?

So Algernon parted from her that evening in a state of exaltation; but it lasted only long enough for her to get out of sight, then down, down he plunged into a bottomless pit of despair. He was one of the unfit, and she had rejected him, and what was there for him to live for any longer? It seemed to poor Francis-Edward as if the whole world had suddenly become a dessert. He stared about him in terror, marveling at the emptiness of his life. His whole being had been so transfused with the thought of Lois that now when he realized that he was to be separated from her he could not imagine what he was to do. Every thing reminded him of her, every place where they had been, everything that he had to do, every topic about which he thought. How cruel it seemed that she should go her way, would interest herself in other matters, and perhaps forget all about him! How cruel it seemed that he should care so much for her, and she should care nothing for him! All night he wrestled with himself, and when she saw him in the morning, he was pale, agitated, and trembling. He would not say another word, he would try to be brave and to behave himself, but she read his grief in his eyes, and her heart was full of pity for him.

They went for a sail again, and she said, I think I ought to go away."

"Ah, don't say that!" cried Algernon. "I am not doing any harm!"

"I know," she said, "but you have got to forget me and get yourself together, and there is no use putting it off."

"I can be happy just seeing you!" he exclaimed.

But she shook her head; she did not believe that.

"Some day," she said, "we can be friends, but now while you feel about me as you do at present. I ought to go away."

And that was her decision. "I will talk it over with mother," she said, "and arrange to go somewhere else, and you must not follow me."

"You have told your mother about me?" he inquired.

Lois laughed, "No," she said, "and for Heaven's sake don't you tell her!"

Algernon was puzzled. "Why not?"

"Because," she replied, "my mother has some respect for money, and she would never give me any peace if she knew."

Algernon pondered over this remark. He did not need any explanation; it only made him sadder, because he realized the difference between Lois and other women.

That afternoon she told him that she and her mother and brother were to take a trip through the West Indies upon a steamer which sailed the following morning. How transported with happiness Algernon would have been had he only been permitted to take the party upon this trip on the "Comet"! But he dared not even suggest it. He knew why Lois was taking the trip, and in her quiet and firm, but kindly attitude he read his death.

They went for a sail that evening. Francis-Edward was like a man in a dream, a man who dreads the hour when he must awaken. He dared not let her see the extent of his misery. He sat there, with his hands clenched tightly, staring ahead of him across the water, listening to Lois's voice and choking back the sobs that rose in him. She was very gentle and painfully sensible. She talked to him about his money and what me might do with it. She tried to explain to him some of the problems of human suffering. She made him promise to read books that she would send him. But Francis-Edward heard her vaguely and answered as best he could, and all the time it was all he could do to keep himself from catching her hand, and crying "It is you I want — you!" But he gave no sign. He took her back to the hotel where she was staying; there on the piazza she turned to bid him good bye. Then he could not help himself; he caught her hand in his, bowed his head, trembling, unable to control himself. He dared not trust himself to speak; he pressed her hand to his lips, then turned and rushed away into the darkness which was the beginning of a long and cruel siege for our hero.

He would not go back to the yacht; he went out into the country, and spent the night wondering aimlessly. He said that he could not bear to see her again; but then he decided that he must see her. And so he went and shook her hand again and saw the steamer push off from the dock, and saw her form fade away into the distance. Then he turned back. Where should he go? What should he do? He could not bear the deck of the "Comet," because she had been there once. He could not bear the hotel where she had stayed, the streets upon which she had walked, the boat she had taken him sailing in. He must go away, he told himself, to some place where she had never been. Then he would go and wander off into the country and come back, thinking that at least he must see the places that had power to bring her image before him.

Poor Francis-Edward understood with a new and cruel poignancy the meaning of the symbol of a little god with the bow and arrows: he had been shot, and he went about struck with a mortal wound in his soul. She had left him without one particle of hope; that was the most dreadful aspect of all. She had told him that he must cease to love her, must cease to think about her in that way, and yet he could not make up his mind to give her up. His thoughts would come back to her again and again, to ways by which he might win her, to wild dreams of regaining his health, of proving his power, of showing her that he was more of a man that she imagined. Francis-Edward was very humble, and yet there was a way in which he was proud; there was something within him that insisted that he was not a weakling; it was only that circumstances were against him. He might have grown up to be a man if he had been born as anything else but a rich mans' son.

He looked back upon his whole career in the light of what Lois had taught him; he saw now how wrong, how wicked the whole thing had been. He saw all the vices and the diseases of his ancestors, the unwholesome-ness of their lives, the social waste, and the suffering they had represented; he was the culmination of all their folly and wickedness! It was his fate to atone for it all. Truly, the sins of the fathers were visited on the children to the third and fourth generation!

And now here was Francis-Edward, with a mind suddenly awakened to these things, teaming with new ideas, new hopes and visions. Here he was with a newly discovered power to think, to study, and find a way out of all these miseries, to become the master of his life; and it was all futile, he was condemned to eternal failure and torment — and all because of his wretched, his accursed body! His mind might grow in a series of explosions, but was there any explosion that could be of any help to his stomach? Here, for instance, he was, trying to be brave, trying to take Lois's advice, not to think about himself, to interest himself in some worth while work, trying to read the books that she had given him, and here was his poor body going to pieces again, worse than ever!

Perhaps it was only because Francis-Edward had so many more reasons for wanting to be well that his weakness seemed so much more intolerable to him. Lois had given him a new vision of health as she had of everything else. Handicaps and limitations which before he had taken as a matter of course, had now suddenly become intolerable. He was like a man who is suddenly stung and goaded and roused into action, and for the first time discovers the full power of the chains which bind him to the earth. For so many years Francis-Edward had dragged through his wretched life, content if he could be the tenth part of a man; now he wished to be a complete man, and because he could not be it, his life suddenly took on the aspect of a nightmare, an intolerably wicked thing!

So for three days he wandered about the island like a lost soul. He went out to his yacht and ordered steam up and started for one of the ports where Lois's steamer was to stop; then in shame and agony of spirit he turned back and went ashore again. He got some of the books which she had recommended to him, he tried to read them. He thought about some of the plans she had suggested to him. He tried to picture himself going back to New York, and setting to work to carry these into affect. But he had to think of his doing these things without her, and he was powerless to do it. With her they wore the face of beauty and happiness; without her they were empty skulls. He could not see any of the hope she had held out to him; he could only see the humiliation and despair of his past. He had been rejected; he was one of the unfit. So he writhed and tore at his chains, and only wounded and crippled himself the more. The effect of all this nervous agitation was to almost paralyze his stomach. It went on a strike completely. He scarcely dared to eat anything, and yet he was losing weight so fast that he dared not stop eating. Whenever his stomach behaved like that he would force himself to exercise; but now he wandered about all day, until he was so exhausted that he could hardly stand, and still nothing helped. He wanted Lois.

And of course just as his grief affected his stomach, so his stomach affected his grief. It would have been hard to disentangle the two, and to say which was having the worst effect upon him. After all, was it not because of his stomach that Lois had rejected him? It was only because the accursed stomach would not work that he had not been man enough to win her. He stretched out his hands to the sky and called down imprecations of Heaven upon the head of his infernal stomach.

He had been rejected; he was one of the unfit. He said it over to himself, a thousand times. It became a refrain that haunted him, a fixed idea that cursed him and cast him down into the pit of despair. Yes, he was hopeless; there was nothing to do but to get away and to make way for people who were stronger to cope with the problems of life. He jeered at himself for his imbecility — he wished to marry and have a child! The time came when he could not bear it. In the lonely hours of the night he summoned the spirit of Lois before him, and wrestled it out with her. The responsibility was too much for him, the burden was too heavy; he could not bear it. He would take himself out of the way. He could give her the power which he could not use. She had rejected him; at least she should realize that he had the strength to realize his unfitness and to take himself out of the way. In the midst of one final agonizing crisis of dyspepsia he took his desperate resolve. He would leave all his money to the causes in which Lois was interested, giving her the administration of it, and then he would kill himself.

The idea came to him in a blaze of light; it was the final solution of all his troubles.

It was with relief and even joy that Francis-Edward set about his task when once his mind had been made up. Early the next morning he summoned a couple of lawyers and made a will. He spent many hours consulting with them, getting every detail of it precise and lawyer proof. Francis-Edward was an only child, but he had some uncles and aunts and cousins, and he was not minded that they should profit by his misfortunes. He made several copies of the document and forwarded them to his lawyers in New York, and to Lois at the address she had given him in Havana, and yet an extra copy for safety to her address at home. All of which having been attended to, he drew a sigh of relief and set out for the dock, where he found the boat in which Lois had sailed.

He had decided how he would kill himself. He could not shoot himself or take poison; that would be ugly and it would leave a painful memory for her to dwell upon. No, he would die with her image before him; he would die in the boat which she had consecrated by her presence. He left letters telling what he meant to do, so that there would be no doubt of what had happened to him.

He purchased the boat outright so that he need not have that on his conscience. Without saying a word to anybody, he stepped on board and set out alone down the harbor. He did not know very much about sailing, but he had watched Lois and his task was a very simple one. The harbor was broad and the channel was clear and the breeze was not too strong. The vessel glided along, and Francis-Edward sat at the wheel, his jaws set tight. Out through the harbor's entrance he could see the blue line of the open ocean. There was his destination. He gazed about him at the boat. Every foot of it made him think of Lois in some way. Here was the cushion upon which she had sat. There was the cup out of which she had drunk. There was the magazine which she had read, and thrown away. He remembered her every motion, as she had tended the wheel. He remembered the orders she had given him when he handled the sheet. He looked about him at the harbor; every aspect of that reminded him of her, of things that she had said, emotions that she had felt. He looked ahead once more at the open sea. That too reminded him of her, for it was thither that she had gone. He would follow. He remembered how he had watched the wake of the disappearing steamer. He imagined himself sailing in that wake into eternity he would pursue her.

So all day he sailed. He passed the entrance to the harbor, he went out to sea. The blue line of the horizon opened out before him, and closed in the rear to receive him. The island receded into the distance; it became a faint dark line upon the horizon, it vanished altogether. Francis-Edward was alone upon the sea. He sat and clutched the wheel, staring before him fixedly. The fresh breeze continued, and the little craft sped on and on. Where was he going? He did not know nor care. He was going to sail, to sail forever. Sooner or later would come a storm and the little vessel would be engulfed, or before that happened perhaps he would die of hunger or of thirst, or if the pain of these became disagreeable, one leap into the sea and all would be ended.

The breeze freshened, and the boat sailed on and on. Francis-Edward came back out of his dreams of Lois, to realize that he was hungry. He laughed to himself a grim laugh. He would fool his old stomach this time. It might growl and grumble all it pleased; never more would it make trouble for him. Yes, he thought he would stay on the boat and sail for a while yet; he would have a day or two in which to punish that stomach. A strange sensation it was to be able to tyrannize over his stomach, which for so many years had tyrannized over him. He was as good as dead, so pain had no more meaning to him; he was above it and beyond it. He could laugh at it, that grim sardonic laugh.

It is said that a drowning man recalls all the events of his past life. Algernon sat in the boat and recalled them deliberately. It pleased him to go over each individual spell of sickness; to dwell upon all the separate weaknesses. How petty and unreal they seemed now! What a strange flouting thing was life anyway, which depended upon the welfare of ill-fare of a stomach — and of a liver, and of a few other much strange contrivances! Francis-Edward got a new insight into the effect of the mind upon the body. He got a new and higher vision of Christian Science. Here was a real illustration of the supremacy of the mind. Here was a moment of real freedom, a hand clasp with the infinite. The hungrier Francis-Edward grew, the more it pleased him, It served only as a spur to his exaltation. The hungrier he grew, the funnier was the joke upon his stomach! He laughed aloud; he discussed his stomach before its very face, so to speak. He pointed out to it its misconduct, and that now it was only getting its just deserts.

But of course in an emergency like this Francis-Edward could not devote very much time to a more material thing like a stomach. He only had a short while more to live, and precious emotions were calling him. He would forget that he was hungry, he would be thinking about Lois again. He would be imagining her receiving his letter with a copy of his will; he hoped it would not hurt her too much. He was sure that she would understand; that he had not acted out of anger or with a desire to punish her. And yet he would want her to suffer a little, for he wanted her to realize how he loved her. No doubt she was used to having men make love to her. At least he had done something to get himself apart from the throng; he would live in her memory, he would be useful to her. He found himself making speeches to her, telling her about it, explaining and apologizing to her. He knelt at her foot again and clasped her hands. And now she was no longer indifferent, now she appreciated him. She realized that after all he was a great soul, no petty weakling, as he seemed to that outer eye. For this she honored him; she even loved him. She recognized him as her soul's true mate. He felt her hand return his clasp; he looked up and saw a tear trembling in her eyes, he caught her to him, crying, "Lois, Lois!"

Then the dream would vanish, and he would sit staring out across the sea. The sun was setting; he was sailing directly away from it, sailing into the darkness. It seemed symbolic to him. The horizon before him was clouded in the somber grey; it was like a mist, rising to veil him. It was annihilation closing about him, swallowing him up. He shuddered a little; Oh, why should he have to go alone? If only Lois had been....

Editor's note: As previously mentioned, it is not known if this was an alternative ending to the novel, or if more pages followed this unpublished installment. Lois not only is the only woman Algernon has become infatuated with, but she is also the only person who was not interested in him or his money. However, since the novelette is a satire, it would be reasonable to suspect that it did not end in his suicide. A possible ending to this segment: Lois receives Algernon's will and suicide letter. She quickly summons the captain of his yacht and sails out of the harbor to find him. Algernon has another vision of her; this time he sees the real Lois, who, along with the yacht's crew, rescues him. After he is hauled aboard his boat, she scolds him for not being a real man. She tells him she is not interested in being left anything in his will as she plans to make her own money and her own way in life to further her causes. Algernon then sails back to New York to begin another misadventure.

Bibliography

The bibliography is limited to published works. Unpublished manuscripts and correspondence of the Sinclair Manuscript Collection, Lilly Library, Indiana University, Bloomington, Indiana, are referenced in each chapter.

Ahouse, John. *Upton Sinclair: A Descriptive Annotated Bibliography.* Los Angeles: Mercer & Atchison, 1994.

Arthur, Anthony. *Radical Innocent: Upton Sinclair.* New York: Random House, 2006.

Blinderman, Abraham. *Critics on Upton Sinclair.* Coral Gables, FL: University of Miami Press, 1975.

Brevda, William. *Harry Kemp, the Last Bohemian.* Lewisburg, PA: Bucknell University Press, 1986.

Bloodworth, William A. *Upton Sinclair.* Boston: Twayne Publishers, 1977.

Dell, Floyd. *Upton Sinclair: A Study in Social Protest.* New York: George H. Doran Co., 1927.

Engs, Ruth Clifford. *The Eugenics Movement: An Encyclopedia.* Westport, CT: Greenwood Press, 2005.

_____. *Clean Living Movements: American Cycles of Health Reform.* Westport, CT: Praeger, 2000.

_____. *The Progressive Era's Health Reform Movement.* Westport, CT: Praeger, 2003.

Gottesman, Ronald. *Upton Sinclair: An Annotated Checklist.* Kent, OH: Kent State University Press 1973.

Gottesman, Ronald and Charles L.P. Silet. *The Literary Manuscripts of Upton Sinclair.* Columbus, OH: The Ohio State University Press, 1972.

Harris, Leon A. *Upton Sinclair, An American Rebel.* New York: Thomas Y. Crowell, 1975.

Harte, James Lambert. *This Is Upton Sinclair.* Emmaus, PA: Rodale Press, 1938.

Mattson, Kevin. *Upton Sinclair and the Other American Century.* Hoboken, NJ: John Wiley & Sons, 2006.

Scott, Ivan. *Upton Sinclair: The Forgotten Socialist.* Lewiston, NY: Edwin Mellen Press, 1997.

Sinclair, Mary Craig. *Southern Belle, with a foreword by Upton Sinclair.* New York: Crown Publishers, 1957.

Sinclair, Upton. *The Autobiography of Upton Sinclair.* New York: Harcourt, Brace & Word, Inc., 1962.

_____. *American Outlook: A Book of Reminiscences*. New York: Farrar & Rinehart, 1932.
_____. *The Book of Life*. Girard, KS: Haldeman-Julius, 1922.
_____. *The Fasting Cure*. New York; London: M. Kennerley, 1911.
_____. *Love's Pilgrimage*. New York; London: Mitchell Kennerley, 1911.
_____. "My Cause," *The Independent* (May 14, 1904):1121–1126.
_____."Perfect Health." *The Contemporary Review* 97 (January–June 1910): 429–440.
_____. *Sylvia's Marriage: A Novel*. Philadelphia: John C. Winston, 1914.
Yoder, Jon A. *Upton Sinclair*. New York: Frederick Ungar Co, 1975.

Index

abortion 8, 16, 37–38, 39
abstinence from alcohol, coffee, tobacco 6
alcohol 46, 56, 59, 62
alcoholism 6, 12, 17, 19, 26, 33, 56, 57, 70
American Civil Liberties Union (ACLU) 32
American Outpost 33
Appeal to Reason 13, 14, 31, 32
Arden, Delaware 22
artificial insemination 30, 92, 98
Australia 30, 92
The Autobiography of Upton Sinclair 35

Barrows, Ellen 23, 25
Battle Creek, Michigan 17, 21
Bermuda 17–18, 28
birth control 9, 12, 37, 116
The Book of Life: Mind and Body 32
Boston 33
The Brass Check 24, 32

California 19, 30
Canada 7, 9, 10
Captain of Industry 12
certificates for marriage 103
Christian Science 15, 33, 170
cohabitation *see* trial marriage
The Cry for Justice 29
The Cup of Fury 34
cures 17, 18, 136

Damaged Goods 27
Davis, Winnie 23
dependent women 118
diets 17, 26, 121, 153; fasting 17, 20, 21, 136, 138; milk 20, 136; raw food 18, 20,
22; Salisbury 22; vegetarianism 17, 18, 23
divorce 19, 24, 25, 26, 86–87, 161; of Upton Sinclair 24
dyspepsia 59, 61, 155, 159, 167, 168

Eastern religions 141
emotions and health 146–147
England *see* United Kingdom
Epic Campaign 33
eugenics 27, 40, 44, 91, 92–102, 160, 162, 167, 168
exercise 18

Fabian Society 17
Fairhope, Alabama 21
The Fasting Cure 22
First Families of Virginia 27
Flivver King 34
Ford, Henry 33

Gartz, Kate Crane 31, 34
Germany 25, 26, 27, 29
Good Health and How We Won It 18
The Goose Step 32
The Great War *see* World War I
Gulfport, Mississippi 23, 29

The Health of Little Algernon 13, 22
health regime 128, 136
Helicon Home Community 15
Heron, George 1, 12, 25
Holland 25, 26
Howatt, David 20

illegitimacy *see* unwed motherhood
illness: Craig's illnesses 26, 34, 35; David's illnesses 12, 13; Meta's illnesses

and surgeries 13, 14, 16, 17, 37; Upton's dyspepsia and stomach problems 10–11, 14, 63
independent women 47, 58, 60, 113, 115–116, 158, 164
inherited tendency 57, 93, 162, 166

Jimmie Higgins 31
The Journal of Arthur Sterling 10, 11
The Jungle 14–15, 29

Kellogg, John Harvey 17
Kemp, Harry 18, 20, 21, 23
King Coal 29
Kuttner, Alfred 17, 19, 20, 22, 23

Lanny Budd series 34
Lilly Library 35, 36
London, Jack 12, 33
Love's Pilgrimage 10, 22, 23, 24
Ludlow Massacre 28

Manassas 12, 13
marriage 113, 127; of Upton Sinclair 9, 27, 35; *see also* trial marriage
Mcfadden, Bernarr A. 20
mental healing 18, 33, 37, 138, 139, 147
Mental Radio 33
metaphysics 138, 139, 140–143,
The Metropolis 17
The Millennium 18
The Moneychangers 18, 19
muckrakers and muckraking 27, 31
"My Cause" 12

The Naturewoman 21
New Thought religions 139–140, 141, 142–143
New York City 8–10, 18, 22, 23, 25, 28
nudism 137

Oil! 32
osteopathy 155

the perfect child 40, 163
Physical Culture 20, 21, 22, 25
pregnancy 10
the press 24, 29
Prince Hagen 9, 10, 12
Profits of Religion 25, 31
Prohibition 33
psychic phenomena 33, 107, 140–141

Pulitzer Prize 34
Pure Food and Drug Act of 1906 15

race degeneracy 96
race improvement *see* eugenics
religion and religious organizations 7, 25, 29, 31, 79, 158
Rockefeller, John D. 28
Roosevelt, Theodore 15
Russell, Lady Molly 25

Sacco and Vanzetti trial 33
self publishing 9
sex education 28, 160
sexual and emotional affairs 14, 15–16, 17, 21, 23, 24, 37
sexual double standard 13, 16, 48–49, 76, 78, 84
sexual innocence and ignorance 9, 22, 49–51, 76
sexual relations, lack of 13
sexually transmitted diseases 27–28, 98
Sinclair, David 10, 12, 13, 17, 18, 20, 21, 22, 24, 25, 26, 27, 29, 30, 31
Sinclair, Mary Craig Kimbrough 21, 23, 24, 25, 33, 34, 35
Sinclair, Meta Fuller 8, 9, 10, 12, 14, 15, 16, 17, 18, 19, 21, 22, 23, 24, 25, 29, 35, 39
Sinclair, Upton Beall: early childhood and family background 5–8; life long recreation 8; writings as a teenager 7–8; writings during his twenties 8–14
single parenthood *see* unwed motherhood
Socialism 11, 15, 31, 158, 164
Southern Belle 35
Spiritualism 150–155
Springtime and Harvest 8, 9, 10
Sterling, George 19, 24, 26, 33
stock yards 14
stomach problems *see* dyspepsia
Stopes, Marie 92, 93, 94, 95
suffragette 27, 45, 67, 164
suicide 33, 150, 168, 169
Sylvia 25
Sylvia's Marriage 28

temperance 63
Theosophy *see* New Thought religions
They Call Me Carpenter 31–32
Thunder Over Mexico 33
tobacco 55, 57, 59

trial marriage 26, 111; Sinclair's opinions
on 16, 18, 22, 23, 26
tutor 8, 27, 128;

the unfit *see* eugenics
United Kingdom 25, 26, 27, 30, 46, 51,
82, 92, 96
unwed motherhood 76, 80, 84, 87–88,
93–95, 98

van Eeden, Frederick 25

vegetarianism *see* diet
venereal diseases *see* sexually transmitted
diseases

water cures 136
Wet Parade 33
Williams, Michael 15, 17, 18
Wilshire, Gaylord and Mary 11, 16, 19, 25
woman suffrage 17, 27, 29, 43–44,
45–54, 77, 158
World War I 29, 30, 32, 94